The Empath's Workbook

THE Empath's WORKBOOK

Practical Strategies for Nurturing Your Unique Gifts and Living an Empowered Life

Krista Carpenter, MS

ROCKRIDGE
PRESS

Interior and Cover Designer: Tricia Jang
Art Producer: Samantha Ulban
Editor: Seth Schwartz
Production Editor: Sigi Nacson
Production Manager: Jose Olivera

All images used under license Shutterstock
Author photo courtesy of Andy Bowen

ISBN: Print 978-1-64739-692-3 | eBook 978-1-64739-801-9
R0

For my dear friend Kelly.

There are no words that
adequately express my gratitude for
how you changed my life. Thank you
for your friendship, your unconditional
love, and your constant cheerleading.
You are an angel—and you taught me
that I am one, too. This book would not
have been possible without you.

Contents

Introduction

It can sometimes be excruciating to feel all the things that we empaths do. We commonly feel overwhelmed and sometimes struggle with depression and anxiety. Frequently, my empath clients believe they are going insane due to all the ups and downs they experience. Being an empath can be very isolating and confusing, and it is common for us to second-guess ourselves at every turn. It can be so painful, in fact, that many of us turn to alcohol or drugs to escape from the emotional roller coaster that we unwillingly ride every day.

The Empath's Workbook will help you get off that roller coaster. It will teach you tools, techniques, and tricks to give you more power over what you feel. You will be much more in control of your emotions and your happiness, and you will gain a deeper understanding of and appreciation for yourself.

I have lived the roller coaster ride that most empaths experience. Raised by a narcissistic parent, like many empaths, I struggled with depression and anxiety for years. Eventually, I tried to end the pain with an overdose on prescription medication. I wound up on a respirator, close to death. I recovered and returned home, feeling even worse than I had before my suicide attempt.

In the months that followed, a dear friend and mentor taught me what it meant to be an empath. The more I learned, the more I experimented with my reality. The more I experimented, the more I learned. Within a year, my life had made a 180-degree turn.

I found a way to slow down the emotional roller coaster, to get on and off at will, and even to enjoy the darn thing.

Now, as a licensed professional counselor and certified life coach, I work with the empath community. Most important, I am happy—truly and wildly happy. I am thrilled to present what I have learned both in my personal life and coaching work with you in this workbook. (I have changed all names and identifying information of the clients I describe in this book. All stories pertaining to them are based on actual events, but the details have been altered to respect my clients' privacy.)

When it comes to the empath, words do not teach. Experience is what educates us. For that reason, I strongly encourage you to complete all of the quizzes and activities in this workbook. These exercises invite you to explore your experience, so you can decide for yourself what works best for you to decrease the negative aspects and increase the positives of being an empath. The exercises also allow you to put into practice what you learn in each chapter, boosting your comprehension of the material.

My wish is that you will gain knowledge and empowerment from this book. I also hope it will help you find your bliss and use the gifts that you have been blessed with to enhance your life and the lives of those you care about. If empaths around the world can harness their skills, the world would be an even more incredible place.

You can be happy. You can love yourself. You can make your wildest dreams a reality. I know because I have done it. You've got this, friend.

CHAPTER 1

Empath at Heart

In this chapter I explain the difference between having empathy and being an empath, as well as the difference between highly sensitive people (HSPs) and empaths. The "Are You an Empath?" exercise will help you clarify if you are indeed an empath.

I will also explain what I refer to as empath superpowers, or "the clairs," which are unique intuitive abilities that only empaths possess. Then I will give you a list of the eight different types of empaths and a description of each. Two activities will help you determine what type of empath you are and what your superpowers may be.

EMPATHY AND THE EMPATH

As an empath coach and an empath myself, I am fascinated by the ways in which empaths and empathy can heal the world around us. Empathy is an aptitude that allows us to feel connected with one another and that validates the experiences and emotions of others. When we demonstrate empathy, we heal our family, friends, even strangers, which builds a stronger sense of community. Empathic people have the ability to use empathy, as well as their own unique intuitive gifts, to heal people, the earth, animals, and plants.

Empathy

The word *empathy* comes from the Greek word *empatheia*, which simply means "feeling." It makes sense, then, that empathy is the ability to understand, even experience, what another person is feeling. When you feel empathy, you will sense a low level of sadness for someone else who is experiencing an emotional hurt. If you have ever had a friend go through something terrible, and you felt "bad" for them, you were experiencing empathy. The vast majority of us have this ability to put ourselves in another's shoes and to understand what another is feeling.

Empathy is an extremely important experience. Empathy allows us to understand others, as well as ourselves. We do not go around deliberately hurting other people because we have empathy. It is one thing that keeps our bonds with others strong. Empathy allows for connection, community, and a sense of purpose outside of ourselves.

Empaths

Although feeling empathy allows us to understand another person's experience on an intellectual level, the experience of an empath is drastically different. An empath is able to physically, emotionally, and mentally feel the emotions of others in a way that is identical to what the empath would feel if they themselves were going through those emotions.

For example, when an empath is near a person who is experiencing heartbreak, the empath physically feels that person's emotions in their own body: heaviness in their heart, a pit in their stomach, and the restlessness of their muscles.

Empaths have bodies and minds that are comparable to antennae. They pick up and interpret countless signals that are indiscernible to the rest of us. For example, several scientific studies have found that a grouping of brain cells, called mirror neurons, is hypersensitive in empathic people. This cluster of neurons is activated by a person's pain or other emotion. The research suggests that due to their hypersensitive mirror neurons, empaths feel other people's emotions more deeply than a nonempath.

Besides feeling other people's emotions, empaths feel the intentions and vibrational frequencies of other people. Vibrational frequencies are created by the vibrating cells that make up all things, including people.

Empaths can be any gender, race, or religion. We live all over the world. We come from all socioeconomic backgrounds, and we differ very widely in our traits, personalities, and gifts. Although each empath is unique, empaths often share some common traits, such as introversion, artistic or creative abilities, a deep care for others, finely tuned senses, and sensitivity to the world around them.

Empaths also have abilities that can be called spiritual, intuitive, psychic, or extrasensory. For example, some can sense the history of a place or object without being told. Some empaths feel strongly connected to and can intuitively communicate with animals or plants. Some are human lie detectors. (See "Specific Empath Types" on page 8 for more.) These abilities are what distinguish empaths from people who experience a high degree of empathy and people who are highly sensitive.

Empaths versus Highly Sensitive People

A highly sensitive person (HSP) is someone born with the gift of heightened or more fine-tuned senses. This high sensitivity may be experienced in one or more of the five senses. Psychologist Elaine Aron, who coined the term *highly sensitive person*, estimates that 15 to 20 percent of Earth's population is highly sensitive.

Empaths are HSPs who have extrasensory or intuitive abilities. All empaths are HSPs, but not every HSP is an empath.

Are You an Empath?

Using the following key, please rate your response to the questions below:

 1 = This does not sound like me.

 2 = I sometimes experience this.

 3 = This resonates deeply with me.

1. Have you been called "too sensitive" or "too emotional"? 1 2 3
2. Do you feel other people's emotional or physical pain as though they were your own emotions or physical sensations? 1 2 3
3. Have you ever known that someone was upset without them telling you? 1 2 3
4. Are you kind, considerate, and considered a very good friend to others? 1 2 3
5. Do others seem to come to you to talk or do strangers frequently seem to open up to you? 1 2 3
6. Do you need alone time to feel recharged energetically? 1 2 3
7. Do you sometimes avoid new people or places because they sound too draining? 1 2 3
8. Are you creative, or do you enjoy doing creative things? 1 2 3
9. Is it difficult for you to do things that you don't enjoy? 1 2 3
10. Do you get bored or distracted easily? 1 2 3
11. Does it feel nearly painful to have to listen to small talk because you are really interested in deeper, more meaningful discussions? 1 2 3
12. Can you tell when someone is either lying or being disingenuous? 1 2 3
13. Is it usually difficult to shock or surprise you? 1 2 3
14. Do you enjoy learning about different cultures, rituals, or unique individuals? 1 2 3
15. Do you have any environmental sensitivities (for example, one of your five senses seems to be stronger than other people's)? 1 2 3
16. Do you have an addictive personality? Have you regularly used alcohol, drugs, sex, shopping, eating, or other addictive behavior to cope? 1 2 3

17. Do you pick up on the energy or vibe in certain places? For example, if you are in a building that has a long history, can you pick up on any energy that resides there?   1   2   3

18. Have you ever suddenly had access to information (and just kind of knew it was accurate) even though you have never read about or otherwise learned that information previously?   1   2   3

19. When you witness something cruel, devastating, or traumatic, is it nearly unbearable to watch?   1   2   3

20. Do you have lower back problems?   1   2   3

21. Do you have any issues with digestion?   1   2   3

22. Do you tend to cheer for the underdog or stick up for the disadvantaged?   1   2   3

23. Do you experience feelings of exhaustion or overwhelm, but when you try to sleep, you have trouble?   1   2   3

24. Do you have emotions that seem to emerge out of the blue, or for no reason?   1   2   3

25. Do you feel rejuvenated during/after being near bodies of water such as the ocean, beach, lake, or river?   1   2   3

26. Do you feel more centered while you are in nature?   1   2   3

27. Have you had periods of time where you have felt misunderstood, depressed, or anxious?   1   2   3

28. Do you prefer one-on-one social interactions to group interactions?   1   2   3

29. Do you find yourself blowing up and letting all of your feelings out all at once, rather than feeling or sharing your emotions as they occur?   1   2   3

30. Are you a free spirit? Do you like traveling or experiencing other new things?   1   2   3

31. Do you put other people's needs before your needs?   1   2   3

32. Have you, at any point, been interested in subjects such as psychic abilities, intuition, or alternative healing?   1   2   3

33. Do you have dreams that are so vivid and real that they seem more authentic than reality?   1   2   3

34. Have you ever predicted a future event that did, indeed, come to fruition?   1   2   3

35. Do you love animals, or do animals seem to love you?   1   2   3

36. Have you felt another person's physical complaints—
such as headaches or nausea—in your body?   1   2   3

37. Can you easily pick up on people's intentions?
For example, when you're in a group of people,
can you sense that someone has "bad vibes"?   1   2   3

Enter your total here: _____

RESULTS

37

Your score indicates that you have not experienced the typical things that
many empaths do. However, it is possible that further reading or coaching
may help you gain a deeper understanding of your experience, thus resulting
in a different score.

38–74

You have had some of the same experiences that empaths typically do.
The closer your score is to 74, the more likely it is that you are an empath.
However, it's also possible that instead of being an empath, you are a highly
sensitive person or simply have some of the same natural traits and interests
that many empaths do. It will be helpful for you to continue reading and
practicing the techniques in this workbook, then retake this test. Your score
may change once you are armed with additional information.

75–111

You are very likely an empath. Not every empath will relate to or experience
every item in the quiz, so a higher score does not necessarily mean that you
are a stronger empath. Keep reading and writing in the workbook to gain
clarification on what type of empath you are and how to feel more in control
of your experience as an empath.

EMPATH SUPERPOWERS

Spiritual, intuitive, psychic, or extrasensory abilities—for the sake of this workbook, I will refer to these as *intuitive gifts*. Some empaths have one intuitive gift, and others experience a combination of two or more. There are eight main types of intuitive gifts. I often call them "the clairs."

Clairvoyance. Clairvoyance means "clear seeing." Empaths with this ability receive intuitive information through visions, pictures, or symbols within in the mind's eye. If you can easily close your eyes and see your childhood bedroom, you likely have a knack for clairvoyance.

Claircognizance. Claircognizance is "clear knowing." Empaths with this ability just know things, without prior education or knowledge. For example, you may "just know" that you shouldn't get in the car with your friend Jacob, for no logical or identifiable reason. The following day, you discover that Jacob has been in a car accident. Your claircognizance told you that riding with your friend would not have been safe.

Clairaudience. Clairaudience means "clear hearing." If you are hearing words, whispers, or sounds that are not coming from your environment, it could be that you are hearing messages from spirit guides, loved ones who have passed away, or other invisible sources.

Clairempathy. Clairempathy means "clear feeling." If you have this gift, you have an intense awareness of the emotional states of others, even when there are no indications of the mood readable to others.

Clairsentience. Clairsentience means "clear sensing" and refers mainly to physical feelings. If you have experienced a headache after spending time with a person who has a headache/migraine, it is likely that you are clairsentient.

Clairgustance. Clairgustance means "clear tasting." It means you're able to sense the taste of a food or other substance that isn't physically present. If you experience clairgustance, you might taste the favorite food or drink of a close friend who has passed on, for example. Clairgustance is less common than the other "clairs."

Clairsalience. Clairsalience means "clear smelling." It's the ability to smell a scent that isn't a product of something in the physical environment. One of my empath clients used to walk into my office and smell cigar smoke, even though no one in the office had been smoking one. But a sheriff who smoked cigars had owned and occupied the building many years prior. My client was able to intuitively smell the cigar just as if the sheriff were still there.

Clairtangency. Clairtangency means "clear touch." This is the ability to pick up or discern unseen information connected with an object just by holding or touching that object. While working with an empath to strengthen her clairtangency, I had her hold a piece of my mother's jewelry. Through touch, she sensed that the jewelry had been on Ellis Island and had been passed down through a family. Indeed, my great-grandmother had the locket while she was entering America from Germany, on Ellis Island. The locket had been passed down to my grandmother, and then to my mother.

SPECIFIC EMPATH TYPES

As you can imagine, empaths vary in their personalities, strengths, and intuitive gifts. We can be very different from one another, and each of us experiences the world differently. However, there are some general empath types. These types reflect the typical sensitivities empaths have, the most common kinds of information and energy they pick up on, and the intuitive gifts they possess.

As you read about the empath classifications below, you may recognize yourself in one or more of them. Then again, you might not think you fit neatly into any of these descriptions—and that's just fine.

These classifications are best used as a starting point for comparing your experiences and gifts with those of other empaths. Understanding what types of empaths there are, and which type you most resonate with, can help you begin to build a stronger sense of pride in yourself. This pride, in turn, is a healthy step in your journey from feeling overwhelmed to feeling empowered. You might find that understanding your type can allow for spiritual growth as well.

Physical Empath

Physical empaths feel, in their body, the physical sensations of other people. A physical empath might visit her Aunt June and feel her migraine. Kim Kardashian claims that when she hugs someone, she can tell if they have a cavity. Is it possible that she is a physical empath?

Intuitive Empath

An intuitive empath experiences what others feel without any information being given. They are often good lie detectors, as they have an unusually sharp sense for whether someone has bad intentions, and when someone is lying. I resonate most with the intuitive empath. An example of my experience with this is when my mother was driving me to the airport recently. I could feel her anger at me, but when I asked her about this, she completely denied any anger, and we had a pleasant conversation the rest of the way. When I landed, however, I opened my phone to several texts from her stating that she had indeed been angry with me over something I had said at a dinner the week before.

Earth Empath

Earth empaths are sensitive to the planet and its energies. They sense information about the earth and their environment much like animals do: by feeling subtle energies and natural forces that normally go unnoticed by humans. If there is an impending flood, for example, animals can usually sense it coming before humans do and will seek higher ground. This type of empath will feel the same invisible environmental cues that animals do in this situation. One of my coaching clients, an earth empath, went to Sedona, Arizona, with some friends. As she walked through the small town, she could feel strange but soothing energies in certain spots. Sedona is known to have numerous vortexes, or centers of moving energy from the earth, which assist in healing, meditation, and self-exploration. Although nonempaths may also be able to physically feel such vortexes, an earth empath would be more highly tuned to them.

Fauna Empath

Fauna empaths are also called animal empaths. Such empaths feel a strong connection to animals. They often exhibit an uncanny understanding of animals and communicate one-on-one with animals intuitively. They usually spend as much time as they can with animals, often working in a setting that allows them to care for them. You may have heard of Francis of Assisi, and his unusual skill that allowed him to tame a wolf. The story says that a wolf appeared and began attacking livestock. Soon the wolf graduated to attacking humans, and eventually dined solely on human victims. One day the wolf ran toward Francis with its mouth open, ready to eat. Francis commanded the wolf to stop its attacks, at which point the wolf slowed his pace, and lay at Francis's

feet, putting its head into Francis's hands. I would say, if the story is true, that Francis of Assisi was a fauna empath.

Flora Empath

Flora (or plant) empaths feel a deep relationship with plants, trees, and flowers. Such empaths love growing plants and feel refreshed in gardens. Flora empaths understand what plants need, and can revive plants that to others appear to be a lost cause. I once had a coaching client who called in distress, as she could hear the cries of a tree as her neighbor was cutting it down after a storm. Another client talked about the lovely singing that came from the vegetables and flowers she tended in her garden.

Spiritual Empath

Spiritual empaths are connected to the spiritual realm. They experience the dead, spirits, and other entities from the world most people cannot see. When working with a spiritual empath, I noticed that she took longer to answer questions than most of my clients. When I asked her about this, she stated that before answering, she tuned in to see if her spirit guides were giving her any guidance, before responding. She made me a believer, as she shared some of the things her angels would say. They were always unnervingly accurate, and many times humorous with their delivery.

Precognitive Empath

Precognitive empaths have the power to know the future. Their knowledge comes from dreams, visions, or other intuitive means. Emily, a precognitive empath, had multiple experiences in which she suddenly knew what was about to happen. One example is that she was walking home after a bartending shift, and she began to think she was being followed. She started rushing, and looked all around, but she didn't see anyone. She sat on a bench for a moment, and tuned in to her sensations. She came to the conclusion that it was her friend, Jamie, who was going to be stalked that night. She called Jamie, with no answer. The following day, Jamie returned her call, and shared that a strange man had indeed followed her home and tried to get into her apartment building.

Psychometric Empath

Psychometric empaths can touch inanimate objects and draw impressions or information from them. These empaths may know where an object came from, its significance, and the time from which it originated. My 16-year-old client Jack is a lifeguard. He often finds lost items at the bottom of the pool. More often than not, he can tell you about the objects he finds: "It belongs to a middle-aged woman, and it was given to her by her grandmother. They had a very close bond, and this ring is very important to its owner." Then, as someone would come to the pool searching for what they had lost, Jack would pick up the missing item and hand it over to its rightful owner, before they had even told him what they were looking for.

Exploring the Empath Types

Using a colored pencil or marker, color in the boxes that describe you:

A	B	C	D
I am an animal lover.	I hate small talk.	I can feel another person's physical pain.	I recycle.
I am a vegetarian.	I know when someone is lying.	I would feel sick if I visited a hospital.	I avoid using plastic.
I am a vegan.	I don't like people who are not genuine.	I can sense when an animal is ill.	I feel best in nature.
I own a pet.	I can "read" people.	Sometimes I know things that I have not learned about previously.	I enjoy outdoor adventures.

E	F	G	H
I like gardening.	I have a good sense of what is going to happen, before it does.	I can tell to whom an item belongs by touching it.	I can sense the presence of spirits.
I enjoy flowers.	I have dreams that come true.	I get information about an object when holding it.	In historical buildings, I sense entities from the past.
I have planted a tree.	I have a vivid imagination.	I get impressions from photographs.	I have received a message from someone who has passed away.
I enjoy botanical gardens.	I can close my eyes and imagine an apple.	I just know where objects came from.	I believe that our souls go on after death.

Take a look the tables and see how many boxes you colored in each column. Then use the key below to see what type of empath corresponds with the details of each column. For example, if you colored four boxes in column C, you have many traits of the physical empath type.

Please note that if you have numerous colored boxes spread out in each of the categories, that is also okay. Many empaths have the qualities of multiple empath types.

A = FAUNA/ANIMAL EMPATH
B = INTUITIVE EMPATH
C = PHYSICAL EMPATH
D = EARTH EMPATH
E = FLORA/PLANT EMPATH
F = PRECOGNITIVE EMPATH
G = PSYCHOMETRIC EMPATH
H = SPIRITUAL EMPATH

A JOURNEY OF SELF-DISCOVERY

As we have discussed, empaths have been blessed with many sensitivities and intuitive gifts. Sometimes these traits and abilities can make us feel overwhelmed. In fact, some empaths struggle with how to live a fulfilling and happy life given how deeply they experience things. Addictions, lower back pain, stomach issues, and insomnia are common complaints of empaths who have not yet found the necessary tools to balance their emotions.

Understanding yourself, your sensitivities, and your gifts is important to becoming a happy and empowered empath. *The Empath's Workbook* has been written to help you do just that: learn about yourself, other empaths, and what to do to live your best life.

I recommend rereading this chapter after completing the workbook. You might find that you identify with more of the intuitive gifts of the types of empaths in this section than you had originally thought.

Exploring Your Empath Experience

Take some time to write down your thoughts about what you've learned so far. Specifically address the following:

1. Which of the empath types described in this chapter resonates with you most?

_____

_____

2. How do you think you could use this information to help yourself and others?

_____

_____

3. If you could strengthen your abilities with regard to these empath types, what would you like to be able to do? (For example, would you like to have the ability to talk to the dead?)

_____

_____

4. Based on the empath type(s) you resonate with, what might some of your intuitive abilities be?

_____

_____

5. What aspects of these types are you drawn to most?

_____

_____

6. What would you like to learn about yourself and other empathic people? And what do you hope to gain from this workbook? Write your goals here.

_____

_____

Get to Know Your Senses

It's possible, after reading this chapter, that you already know what your dominant intuitive gift is and what type of empath you are. It is just as likely that you are more confused than ever. This activity will give you more clarity on who you are as an empath.

Weather permitting, go outside in your bare feet, preferably where you have some privacy. If this is not possible, stand barefoot on the floor in your home. Stand tall, and position yourself so your footing would remain solid if someone were to attempt to shove you. Then, take three deep breaths in and out.

Next, look around. Use your five senses to notice what surrounds you. Take at least two minutes to observe your environment. What do you see? What do you taste? What do you hear? What do you feel? What do you smell?

When you feel that you have tuned in to your surroundings, answer the following questions:

1. What did you notice?

_____

_____

2. Were you aware of any sounds that might not have stood out to you normally? If so, what were they?

_____

_____

3. Were you aware of any objects, colors, or other sights? If so, describe them.

_____

_____

4. Did you notice the feel of anything on your face or in your hair such as sun or wind?

_____

_____

5. Were you able to taste anything that was part of your environment? If so, describe your experience.

_____

_____

6. Was there anything else noteworthy about your experience?

_____

_____

Based on your answers and experience, were any of your senses especially robust? Did you have any answers that were significantly longer or more detailed than the others?

If you had one sense that was more dominant, then see if you can pair that with the lists of empath types and intuitive abilities. For example, if your sense of hearing was the most detailed and prevalent, look at the list of empath descriptions and identify which type seems to rely heavily on hearing. Then look at the list of intuitive gifts and see if your experience with hearing during this activity could, theoretically, fit into one of the clairs. Write comments and reflections here.

_____

_____

_____

_____

_____

Reflect on or write down any other instances when, in hindsight, you had especially strong sensations. Have you had any past experiences in which one of your five senses was strong or noteworthy? Have you had any past times where you were able to receive some information or knowledge, but didn't know where it came from? These are all clues that will help you determine which type of empath you are and which intuitive gifts may be your strongest.

_____

_____

_____

_____

_____

Over the next several days, pay attention to your strongest sense and clair. Write down any experiences that occur in regard to either or both of these. Is it possible that a message was being given to you? If so, what was the message?

_____

_____

_____

_____

_____

With some attention and practice, the type of empath that best fits you will emerge. As you complete this workbook you will also gain some insight into your strongest intuitive gifts.

KEY LESSONS AND REFLECTION

→ All empaths experience and show empathy, but not everyone who experiences empathy is an empath.

→ All empaths are highly sensitive people, but not all HSPs are empaths.

→ Each empath has gifts and abilities that are unique to them.

→ The eight main intuitive gifts are: clairvoyance, claircognizance, clairaudience, clairempathy, clairsentience, clairgustance, clairsalience, and clairtangency.

→ Some specific types of empath are physical, intuitive, earth, fauna, flora, spiritual, precognitive, and psychometric.

→ To be happy and healthy, empaths must learn about their sensitivities and gifts.

Reflection Questions

1. Were you surprised by anything you learned in chapter one?

_____

_____

_____

_____

_____

2. Was there anything you read that brought up memories from your past that could have been explained as an intuitive gift? What were they?

_____

_____

_____

_____

_____

3. At this point, what type of empath would you say you are?

_____

_____

_____

_____

_____

4. What topics from this chapter would you like to come back to later?

_____

_____

_____

_____

_____

Empath in the World

Chapter two focuses on some of the challenges empaths commonly deal with. Absorbing too much emotion and energy, feeling overwhelmed by groups or crowds, and loneliness are common complaints from empathic individuals.

This chapter will help you with these issues by teaching you three things: how to improve your boundaries; how to protect yourself from toxic people, such as energy vampires and narcissists; and how to shift your focus from struggling as an empath. Once you learn how to better protect yourself, you can begin to concentrate on the wide variety of benefits of being an empath who feels deeply.

ENERGETIC OVERLOAD

My client Sarah, whom I have always seen as extremely grounded and put together, recently admitted to feeling anxious and overwhelmed "all of the time." I introduced her to the idea that she might be feeling other people's "vibrations," or energies. As she explored what it was like for her to feel the vibrations of everyone she comes in contact with during her day, it became apparent to both of us that she was feeling overwhelmed and anxious not because she was an inherently anxious person, but because she was picking up on all of the vibes of people around her. She was in constant contact with others: people at her office, strangers she crossed paths with while running errands, other drivers during her commute, and her own three children.

Sarah had never before considered that her sensory inputs were stronger and more deeply attuned to the energies of others. It was incredibly empowering for her to realize that that might be what was causing her to feel overwhelmed. Instead of identifying herself as neurotic and anxious, she learned it was possible to "shake off" other people's energies, including their emotional energy, and feel calm and grounded.

Judith Orloff, MD, a leader in the field of the empath experience, says that empaths have an extremely sensitive neurological system. We do not have the same filters to block out stimulation that others have. As a result, we absorb the energies—positive and negative—around us. Being an empath is great once you learn a little more about how to determine what is your energy and what is not.

Epsom and Sea Salt Bath

Feeling overwhelmed with other people's energies? This recipe is my go-to when I need to feel better fast. I call it the "Happy Empath Bath." It helps the body get rid of other people's energy and alleviates any negative energetic remains.

Ingredients

1 cup Epsom salt

½ cup baking soda

½ cup pink Himalayan sea salt

1. In a bathtub, dissolve the ingredients in about 3 inches of extremely hot water. Mix periodically for 5 to 10 minutes, until the granules are mostly dissolved. Then add water until the bath is your desired temperature.

2. For full effectiveness, stay in the Happy Empath Bath for a minimum of 20 minutes, allowing the ingredients to properly absorb through your skin and pull toxins out. Remember to submerge the back of your head, as the base of the head and back of the neck are the major energy centers where we absorb energy.

3. Always finish with a warm rinse of water after your Happy Empath Bath. The Epsom salt can be very drying if excess is left on the skin. Additionally, rinsing assists in shedding the toxins/impurities that the Happy Empath Bath has pulled from your body.

Using Binaural Beats to Reduce Overwhelm and Increase Relaxation

In 1839, a man named Heinrich Wilhelm Dove discovered that different sound tones have different physical effects in the body. Binaural beats are tones that have two different frequencies. One is heard in the right ear, one in the left. The brain interprets these as only one frequency. This frequency can improve how we feel.

There are studies suggesting that listening to binaural beats can change a person's emotions, behavior, and sleep states. Specifically, studies have shown that listening to binaural beats can decrease anxiety, increase concentration, stimulate creativity, improve sleep, decrease stress, and reduce levels of cortisol in the body, among other benefits.

To listen to binaural beats, you only need Internet access and a set of headphones. Music or nature-sound tracks with binaural beats are available for purchase at most online music stores. I use YouTube to find binaural beats, both because they are free, and because I am able to search for beats that are produced specifically for my current need: sleep induction, for example.

For this exercise:

1. Identify your current need. Examples might be that you want an improved mood or decreased anxiety. Maybe you want to recover from a breakup, or enhance your intuitive abilities.
2. Access YouTube via your Internet browser or using the YouTube app on your smartphone or tablet.
3. In the YouTube search bar, type in the words "binaural beats" and your need: "improve mood," "decrease anxiety." If you cannot find binaural beats for your specific need, look for the option that most closely matches your need or try to find one that addresses something else you would like to see improved in your life.
4. Select the result that most closely matches the need you've identified.
5. Put in your headphones, press play on the audio track, and relax.

If you do not have time to relax, or you just like to multitask, you can play binaural beats through headphones as you do other things. You do not need to focus on the binaural beat or the sound of the music. You are free to go about your business as you would normally do.

A few caveats:

→ Do not listen to binaural beats tracks while driving or operating any kind of heavy equipment.

→ Empaths who are sound sensitive may find binaural beats overstimulating. I've also had one client say binaural beats elicited anger in her.

→ If you have epilepsy or a seizure disorder, please consult your primary care physician before listening to binaural beats.

→ If you try listening to binaural beats and experience any uncomfortable or undesirable effects, or if you simply don't enjoy them, trust your experience and don't listen to them again.

ABSORBING TOO MUCH EMOTION

When you feel emotions more deeply than others do, are highly attuned to your five senses, *and* feel the emotions and energies of all the people around you, it can feel extremely overwhelming. Many untrained empaths experience depression, anxiety, and/or suffer with various addictions. This is certainly understandable, as they are experiencing an immense amount of emotion and energy on a continual basis.

Empaths frequently come to my office and say that they were doing fine all day, but then *boom*, like a ton of bricks, their mood went to a sad or dark place, and they wanted nothing more than to escape themselves. Often when this occurs, the empath is feeling an emotion that does not belong to them. This sudden change in their mood is actually a result of the empath coming into contact with someone or someplace that had a sad/dark mood or energy. The empath then felt that energy, and mistook it for their own. Empaths feel, in their mind and body, the feelings of others. Experiencing other people's emotions can seem *exactly* the same as if we are feeling our own emotion. Thus the untrained empath cannot always determine the difference between their emotions and the emotions coming from others. This can be a scary experience, and many of us have felt like we were going crazy as a result.

Good news: Empaths are not doomed to experience this sudden change in moods for the rest of their lives. With the tools provided in this workbook, you will be able to tell the difference between your emotions and other people's. You will be able to turn your sensory inputs up and down, and you will feel better than you ever have!

The next exercises are techniques that can keep you from absorbing too much emotion from other people.

Eggshell Visualization

I abhor going into crowded stores to shop. I used to leave them feeling irritable and overwhelmed due to the various emotions and energies around me. Luckily, I have devised a technique that allows me to leave the house.

When I park my car outside a store, I take about 60 seconds to breathe deeply and imagine a giant eggshell around me. Why this choice of container? An eggshell is covered with as many as 17,000 tiny pores that allow air and water in, *and* it has a coating inside the shell that is impervious. Nothing at all can penetrate the egg: no bacteria, no germs, no emotions from other people! Thus I can breathe, drink water, easily peck out a window or door, *and* my energetic eggshell keeps out the energies of all the screaming babies and weirdos.

To try the eggshell visualization yourself:

1. **Visualize an eggshell around your body.** If the eggshell image is unappealing, simply choose a different container. Imagine a wooden box, a white light, or your spirit guides surrounding you in protection.
2. **Imagine yourself inside your container.** Does it feel just right? If not, what adjustments do you want to make so it is perfect? Maybe you need a window, or maybe you need two containers. Take the time to make any changes so it feels just right.
3. **When your intuition tells you that the container is just right, hold the image of you inside your container for 60 to 120 seconds.** Concentrate on the container, its shape, color, permeability, and other qualities.
4. **Take some deep breaths and try to feel the emotion that is associated with your newfound safety from the emotions of others.** For some it may be a sense of calm; for others it might be excitement at this fresh protection technique.

Use this method before entering a crowded store or before interacting with a negative person. Then, as you do your shopping or other task, remind yourself that you are protected, and that you are not allowing other people's moods or energies inside your container at this point in time. I often reimagine my container two or three times as I am grocery shopping, because it helps me to stay relaxed. Rejoice, as you now have a way to turn down the volume on your sensitivity.

DEEPER PRACTICE:
CORD CUTTING

Everywhere we go, we come into contact with other people. Maybe we bump into a stranger on the sidewalk. Maybe someone tells you their life story at a café. Or maybe we have a social exchange with a friend over lunch. All of these interactions form energetic connections to the individuals with whom we were in contact. For empathic people in particular, others tend to energetically connect with us, as they can sense that we care deeply for others. These people often connect energetically to us when they are in poor physical or emotional health.

Cord cutting is necessary when we would like to eliminate the connection that has formed between ourselves and someone else. Here is an exercise on how to cut energetic cords.

1. Get comfortable in a seated position. It is important to choose an area that is quiet, where you will not be disturbed or interrupted.
2. Visualize the energy that naturally resides in and around your body.
3. Now imagine the cord that runs between you and a person with whom you have been in contact. This cord should be one that you would like eliminated. Some cords may look like fishing line, and others like thick, umbilical-like tethers. The way the cord looks is an indicator of how strong, and how toxic, the energetic connection is.
4. Visualize yourself holding a tool that you will use to cut this cord. It could be scissors, a blowtorch, a razor blade, or dynamite. Use whatever feels like the most appropriate instrument.
5. Visualize using the tool to cut the cord between you and the other person. This may be fast, if the cord is thin. If the cord is thicker or more resilient, this visualization may take longer.
6. Either during or after your visualization, say out loud something like: "I now release this cord that does not serve the interest of my highest self."
7. Take three deep breaths, and come back to the room when you are ready. Repeat this process as you see fit.

PEOPLE OVERLOAD

Empaths are often introverted. For most empaths, spending time around other people can be draining. Feeling the emotions of others can be confusing, exhausting, and overwhelming. Social interaction generally takes a lot of energy for the empath. Being around people all day, which many of us are, considering our jobs, family, and friends, is tiring. Even if your day is filled with positive and uplifting people, it takes a great deal of energy to interact with others, especially for long periods of time, or in group settings.

It is crucial that empaths get some alone time on a daily basis. This prescription may, initially, sound excessive. I like to use the example of a car to explain the reason to clients. Cars need gasoline in order to drive you from place to place. You would never expect your car to take you to work if the gas tank was completely empty. Empaths, in this metaphor, are the cars. Alone time is the gas. Empaths need alone and/or quiet time to fill up their gas tank. They frequently expect themselves to run on empty and become exhausted and miserable as a result.

Or you can think about it this way: A 20-minute self-care routine that you do on a daily basis adds up to 140 minutes, or 2.33 hours, of self-care time per week. Compare this with no self-care time during the week but feeling so depleted on Saturday that you spend 12 hours in bed. Alone time allows empaths to fill their gas tanks, giving them more energy for the days ahead.

How to Handle Crowds with Ease

Being around only one person is potentially draining to the empath. It makes sense, then, that groups of people can be absolutely exhausting. As much as we may want to, we simply cannot turn down every invitation to family holidays, weddings, birthday parties, and other group activities.

Below are some strategies that will help you deal with crowds or groups of people, while remaining grounded. Place an X in the box next to each strategy that you have tried before. After going through the list of strategies, note the ones that you have not yet tried. Set an intention to try some of these new strategies the next time you are in a group setting.

- ☐ Prior to attending a group event, get centered by doing a five-minute meditation, or listen to something uplifting (podcast, speech, or music).
- ☐ Choose carefully next to whom you sit or stand. Do your best to sit close to a person or people whom you know to be calm or positive.
- ☐ If you begin to feel overwhelmed, excuse yourself and go to the bathroom. Enjoy the solitude for a few minutes.
- ☐ Prior to the gathering, inform the host and other guests, if appropriate, that you have to leave at a certain time. That way, if your book club is still going strong after four hours, nobody will be expecting you to stay.
- ☐ Bring water to stay hydrated. Dehydration can cause feelings of anxiousness: Rapid heartbeat, rapid breathing, dizziness, irritability, and confusion are common side effects of dehydration, so it is important for empaths to stay hydrated.
- ☐ Avoid draining conversations when possible. If you don't want to talk to someone, avoid eye contact, don't respond with anything more than an "umm hmm," or just walk away. Strangers tend to tell their life story to empaths with a willing ear.
- ☐ Start a conversation with someone whom you know and like, or someone new you are curious about. The idea is to focus on the conversation and tune out the other sensory stimuli.
- ☐ Help steer the group away from things such as gossip, illness, and intense political debates. One tip is to find a positive aspect related to the topic, and state it so the entire group can hear you. This is intended to dissuade the continuation of negative talk.

- ☐ Breathe. Periodically pause to take three deep breaths during the gathering. Nobody will be able to see you doing so, but it will help you relax and stay centered.
- ☐ Have self-care planned for right before or after the gathering. Spend 20 minutes reading a great book prior to attending, or go home and take a soothing bath afterward.
- ☐ Only commit to social activities if the rest of your day and week look manageable. For example, if you work 40 hours a week and have volleyball practice on Monday, an AA meeting on Tuesday, and a concert on Wednesday, do not commit to attending a group activity on Thursday.
- ☐ Schedule something self-care related to look forward to after the event: a massage, a movie, time for a hobby, a vacation.

LONELINESS

Because most empaths need time alone, especially when we feel overwhelmed, we commonly isolate ourselves a bit more than other people do. This isolation can sometimes lead to loneliness. Empaths also commonly tell me that they feel like no one understands them, which only serves to exacerbate their feelings of loneliness and social isolation. It's important for empaths to have strategies for avoiding loneliness, so that their alone time can be truly restorative.

Tips for Reducing Loneliness

Read each tip for reducing loneliness and then answer the questions that follow.

1. **Stay off social media.** Numerous studies show that social media increases our feelings of social isolation and separation from others.

    What could you do with the time that you usually spend on social media? Are you willing to experiment with these alternatives for one week?

    _____

    _____

2. **Get a pet.** Dogs are man's best friend for a reason! Pets have a calming effect on their owners, and provide a sense of companionship. A 2015 study demonstrated that keeping crickets as pets had a positive effect on older adults. Yes, even pet crickets were shown to decrease depression and loneliness.

    Could you get a pet? If not, where could you volunteer with animals? Could you offer to walk or babysit someone else's pet?

    _____

    _____

3. **Reconnect with friends, family, neighbors, or coworkers with whom you have relationships.** In-person communication is best for eliminating feelings of loneliness, but online services like FaceTime or Skype are also helpful. If your relationships are more that of acquaintances, then put a bit of effort into deepening the ones that interest you most.

    With whom could you have coffee? Is there someone you haven't talked to in a few months who might like to hear from you? Are there any acquaintances you could get to know better?

    _____

    _____

4. **Do some narrative therapy.** Narrative therapy is a method of psychotherapy that focuses on separating a person from their problem. Narrative therapy teaches us how to change the way we see situations, and opens some room for other, more helpful stories. Rewrite the story you are telling yourself. Rather than identifying as lonely, start to tell yourself that your solitude is good. See loneliness through the eyes of an eternal optimist: Alone time is an opportunity for self-care, reflection, and not having to answer to others.

Could I start to see my loneliness differently? How might I refer to solitude in a more positive way?

SETTING BOUNDARIES

Empaths have the tendency to put the requests, demands, and needs of others above their own. For example, imagine you spent Saturday doing things that drained you: grocery shopping in a busy market, getting your oil changed at the same time as everyone else in the city, and standing in line at the bank. You finally get home, put away your groceries, and take off your shoes. The phone rings, and it's your friend Tanya, who is requesting that you help her move out of her apartment tonight and tomorrow, because her other friends bailed on her at the last minute. If you are an empath with little experience setting boundaries, you would probably help Tanya move, even though you really needed the relaxing and quiet time you had planned for after a draining day.

Empathic people have a difficult time saying no, setting healthy boundaries, and asking for their needs to be met. From birth, empaths grow up familiar with their gifts, and have the tendency to assume that *all* people have the same gifts. Thus empaths often assume that other people *just know* when the empath needs something. In reality, other people do not just know this information. Empathic people need to communicate their needs to others for this reason.

Humans have numerous types of boundaries including physical, mental, emotional, and spiritual. Emotional boundaries serve two important purposes: They keep us from taking on the emotions of other people, and they keep us from imposing our emotions on others. Empaths generally need to work on having strong emotional boundaries over the course of their lifetime. As you can imagine, this type of boundary is especially difficult for the empath because they feel the emotions of others. They do not, however, have to own those emotions as their own.

One example of a physical boundary is your bedroom. This is where you sleep, likely where you allow yourself to be most vulnerable. The walls of your bedroom draw a physical boundary that says "do not come in," unless of course, your bedroom door is open. Another physical boundary is the invisible bubble that surrounds each of us. When someone crosses that physical boundary we may experience an uncomfortable or "yucky" feeling.

Mental boundaries are what allow us to form our own thoughts and opinions, rather than just believe anything anyone tells us. These boundaries also allow us to discern our own thoughts from other people's thoughts. People with healthy mental boundaries can have respectful, calm political discussions with others. Imagine that: two people talking at a normal volume, respecting each other's opinion, simply sharing information and ideas.

Spiritual boundaries allow you to form a personal relationship with whatever you choose to call God: universe, Mother Nature, source energy, for example. Healthy spiritual boundaries allow us to explore our beliefs about creation, life, death, and spirit. Someone with healthy spiritual boundaries will not allow others to define their relationships with religion, spirituality, or their intuitive gifts.

In working with HSPs and empaths, I have come to understand that one of the most important things a person can do to be a thriving empath is to develop healthy boundaries in all four of these areas: physical, mental, emotional, and spiritual. Although scary at first, I find that once an empath sets a boundary just a couple of times, it gets easier quickly. Sometimes friends or family respond poorly, possibly because they are not used to you setting such boundaries. However, if you continue to do so, they will adjust, and begin to respect your time, opinions, space, and other boundaries.

Learning to put yourself first is a challenge for the empath. I tell all of my clients that their needs are just as important as everyone else's. Each of us is responsible for taking care of our needs, or for asking others for help when we need it. There is an old saying that goes: The trees that are most cared for bear the best fruit. So it is with the empath: Those who care best for themselves have the most to offer others.

Identifying Your Wants and Needs

Before you can set healthy boundaries, you will need to be able to identify what your wants and needs are! This section will help you do just that.

Over the next week, set an alarm to notify you three times each day. Choose times when you are able to take two minutes away from whatever you are doing to check in with yourself. When your alarm rings, ask yourself the following questions:

1. Do I **want** anything right now?
2. Do I **need** anything right now?
3. Can I meet my own wants/needs, or do I need to **ask for help**?
4. If I do need help, **who could I ask**?

You may want to write down anything that comes up emotionally for you as you think about your wants and needs. Use this space to write down some of your wants and needs from the week:

How to Set Healthy Boundaries

Do the following exercise only after you've done the previous one.

Having healthy boundaries includes identifying your wants and needs, saying no, and making requests to others. Over the next week, practice setting boundaries in a few different ways.

Below is a chart where you can record the following: saying no, identifying what you want, identifying what you need, and making a request of someone (in relation to your wants/needs). For example:

DAY 1	
Say no	*When asked to make dinner for my family and my daughter's two neighborhood friends, I said no.*
What do I want?	*At noon, I wanted something sweet. I allowed myself to eat a cookie.*
What do I need?	*After a stressful day, I needed alone time, and a bath to relax.*
I asked for my need to be met by	*I asked my husband to help the kids with homework so I could take a bath and be alone.*
Outcome	*So much better after the bath. Husband was happy that I was relaxed.*

Record your experiences in the corresponding boxes, and under "outcome" make a note about whether setting each boundary was a positive or negative experience for you.

DAY 1	
Say no	
What do I want?	
What do I need?	
I asked for my need to be met by	
Outcome	

DAY 2

Say no	
What do I want?	
What do I need?	
I asked for my need to be met by	
Outcome	

DAY 3

Say no	
What do I want?	
What do I need?	
I asked for my need to be met by	
Outcome	

DAY 4

Say no	
What do I want?	
What do I need?	
I asked for my need to be met by	
Outcome	

Say no	
What do I want?	
What do I need?	
I asked for my need to be met by	
Outcome	

Say no	
What do I want?	
What do I need?	
I asked for my need to be met by	
Outcome	

Say no	
What do I want?	
What do I need?	
I asked for my need to be met by	
Outcome	

ENERGY-DRAINING INTERACTIONS: ENERGY VAMPIRES AND NARCISSISTS

As we have discussed, being around other people can be a bit draining for the empath. There are two types of people that are especially exhausting: the energy vampire and the narcissist. Let's take a look at each.

An energy vampire is anyone who seems to suck the life out of you, after time is spent with that person. Energy vampires often have very low vibrations, negative emotional states, see themselves as victims, and have little or no empathy. They will consistently gossip, or pick people apart. They feed on people who will listen, engage in conversation, or those who feel sorry for them. Energy vampires are individuals who take from others, and rarely or never give anything back.

Twenty percent of the population is an energy vampire of some sort, says Dr. Christiane Northrup in her book *Dodging Energy Vampires*. These vampires include narcissists, sociopaths, people with borderline personality disorder, and people with histrionic personality disorder. It is important to note that not everyone with these diagnoses or labels is an energy vampire. It is only a percentage of people that fits into these diagnostic categories who is also an energy vampire.

A narcissist is also especially draining for the empath and can be harder to detect than the energy vampire. Narcissistic individuals believe that they are the center of the world and have an inflated ego. They need a lot of attention, admiration, and praise. They are entitled individuals who use other people to meet their own needs. Narcissists are unable to handle any criticism, because underneath their air of superiority lies an incredibly low self-worth.

Narcissists are extraordinarily manipulative and tend to be skilled liars. It can be difficult to spot a narcissist for that reason. Narcissists frequently engage in what is called "love bombing": They morph from someone very scary to an overly affectionate, adoring, and flattering person, in an attempt to win you over. They will buy you gifts, give excessive compliments, do unnecessary favors, and be at your beck and call. Their love bombing makes the empath feel safe, loved, and appreciated, but this sets up the empath for a huge disappointment.

Narcissists transform from the perfect mate, boss, or friend to someone who is abusive and demanding. The narcissist's goals are to make themselves feel better through devaluing of others, and to make you stick around, in hopes that their abusive behavior is temporary. They want you to believe that the love bombing version is the "real" them.

Do You Know Any Energy Vampires?

It is safe to say that we have all met an energy vampire. In all likelihood, there is at least one energy vampire in each of our lives. Avoiding these individuals is not always possible. They may be family members, coworkers, or neighbors. Below is a quiz that will help you determine if you are indeed dealing with an energy vampire.

1. Does this person tell you more information about themselves than they should, based on the extent of your relationship?
2. Do you dread interacting with this person?
3. Do you ever feel criticized by this person?
4. After interactions with this person, do you feel the need to drink, use drugs, overeat, or isolate?
5. Do you experience stomach pain, headaches, or muscle tension during/after interacting with this person?
6. Do you feel anxious, agitated, or irritable after interacting with this person?

If you answered yes to four or more questions, you are likely dealing with an energy vampire.

How to Protect Yourself from an Energy Vampire

We all need strategies to protect ourselves from energy vampires, and it is especially important for the empath to have protective strategies because energy vampires often target them due to their loving and giving nature.

Recognize the Common Characteristics of an Energy Vampire

Think about a person who you believe may be an energy vampire. Next, place an X in the box next to any characteristics listed here.

- ☐ They diminish your problems and focus on their own.
- ☐ They always try to one-up you.
- ☐ They use your kindness against you.
- ☐ They are codependent (they rely on you to excess for their emotional needs).
- ☐ They criticize, bully, or gossip.

- ☐ They intimidate.
- ☐ They gaslight (manipulate you into questioning your sanity).
- ☐ They are manipulative.
- ☐ They are unable to admit their mistakes.
- ☐ They lie.
- ☐ They give ultimatums.
- ☐ They guilt-trip you.
- ☐ They play the victim.
- ☐ They are always involved in some sort of drama.

If you checked off five or more of the common characteristics, you are likely dealing with an energy vampire. Here are some tips to protect yourself:

1. **Put yourself and your needs first.** The energy vampire will expect you to meet their needs without considering yours. Make sure that you are aware of what your needs are, and make those a priority above all else.

2. **Set boundaries.** Setting boundaries with an energy vampire is a great way to protect yourself.

3. **Get support from a therapist or coach who has experience working with people who have character defects.** In short, character defects are a person's thoughts, words, or actions that they continue to do even though they know they are immoral or harmful to others.

4. **Get a reality check.** If you are unsure about who is an energy vampire, have a friend give you a reality check. Ask your friends to tell you what they think of anyone you suspect of being an energy vampire. You may have to give your friend permission to be brutally honest.

5. **Distance yourself.** If at all possible, distance yourself from the energy vampire. Even if it's a close friend or family member, you cannot have a healthy relationship with someone who expects a one-sided relationship with you.

6. **Use the gray rock technique.** With this technique you become unresponsive or boring. You virtually become like a rock, resulting in the energy vampire losing interest in you. (See the Resources section for the link to a video on this technique.)

Remember the energy vampire that you brought to mind in the beginning of this activity, and answer the following questions:

1. Is there a way for you to either cut off contact with this person, or to distance yourself? If so, how might you go about achieving this?

_____

_____

2. What would be different in the way you interact with this person, if you used the gray rock method?

_____

_____

_____

3. Name three people whom you trust to give you a reality check, when needed.

_____

4. If your best friend were to pick out your three weakest boundaries, what would those be? If you are unsure, ask your friend.

_____

_____

_____

5. Do some research on coaches or therapists who have a good understanding of character defects and energy vampires. It is best to be proactive. You can always come back to this section to easily find a coach, if you should need one. Write their contact information here.

_____

_____

_____

DEEPER PRACTICE:
TAKE BACK WHAT'S YOURS

When an energy vampire or other toxic person takes from an empath, we feel drained and exhausted. Try this ritual to take back your positive energy.

What You Will Need for the Ritual

→ Sage, palo santo, sweetgrass, cedar, or other energetic cleansing herb. Smudging sticks can be found on Amazon or at a natural grocery store.

→ A white candle

→ Black tourmaline, Boji stone, red jasper, or other grounding stone of your choice

→ This workbook and a pen/pencil

Start the ritual by clearing your space of existing energy by using the cleansing herb of your choice.

To smudge a space, light the herbs or stick, and let the flame die out so it is only smoking. You may have to light it several times as you walk through your space. Begin at the front of your space, and move slowly around the space, directing the smoke up and down the walls. Move mindfully around the space, allowing the smoke to get into closets and other dark spaces. When you have covered the space that you wanted to smudge, make sure that the herbs or smudge stick is put out.

Next, light a candle in the center of your space. Say the following, out loud: "I light this candle for my highest self. Let its fire cleanse any pollutions from my body, mind, and spirit."

Hold your grounding stone or crystal as you tune in to your emotional, physical, and energetic sensations. As you focus on yourself, say out loud, "I call back my energy. I call back my power. I call back my vitality."

You can add any other sentences that are personally relevant to you. The last time I called back my energy, for example, I added, "Any negative or painful energies are not welcome here. I ask you to leave now." I repeated all of these sentences about twenty times. The number of times you repeat the sentences is not important; more important is that you can feel a positive shift in your emotional, physical, or energetic sensations.

Continue holding your stone or crystal and repeating your chosen sentences with determination until you feel this shift.

Next, visualize your life force or energy returning to you. Hold your energy, now that it has returned, and breathe deeply. Feel that energy integrate back into your body. Feel it balance and ground you. Feel your vitality rise. Then, say out loud, "I am in control of where my energy goes, and who I share it with."

Take a few minutes to journal about your experience with this ritual. Did it make you feel better, and how so? Would you change anything about the ritual to make it more effective for you? Who has taken some of your energy in the past? How do you feel when this happens? How can you reduce the amount of energy that is taken from you by others?

_____

_____

_____

_____

_____

_____

_____

_____

THE BENEFITS OF BEING AN EMPATH

Despite the challenges of being an empath, there are countless benefits of being highly attuned to other people's energies and having highly sensitive senses. It is key for empaths to be aware of how their sensitivities and abilities can benefit them.

One of my clients was so highly attuned to his surroundings that when he went hiking, he could sense when a bear or mountain lion was getting close. This sensitivity allowed him to turn around and leave the area, avoiding a possible animal attack. Another client with whom I recently worked had a very strong sense of smell. She found it to be annoying, having to deal with perfumes, body odors, and other smells.

However, while camping with her family, her husband opened up a bag of chips and a jar of guacamole. As Julie brought a guacamole-covered chip to her mouth, she could smell that it had gone bad. She was able to prevent an outbreak of food poisoning on the first evening of their family camping trip.

Each empath has a set of gifts that is unique to them. Just like there are no two people who are identical (with the exception of twins), there are no two empaths who have the same skill sets. Each empath will experience different advantages, as each empath is unique in regard to which senses are most delicate, which types of empath they may identify as, and which intuitive gifts (the clairs) resonate with them.

The Gifts of Feeling Deeply

In my coaching work, my clients typically start out seeing their ability to feel things deeply as a curse. However, the trained empath (often called "empowered empath") realizes that although they do feel negative things more deeply, they have the capacity to feel positive emotions intensely as well. How wonderful it is to experience belly laughs, the smell of a newborn baby, or to let the excitement of vacationing fill your entire body! Empaths feel love like no other. They feel peace, gratitude, and joy, on a level others cannot. Empowered empaths are often the happiest people I know.

Some empaths in relationships have a connection that's so deep and powerful that they can feel when their partner is going through something important, even while they are miles apart. Being this sensitive also allows empaths to have an understanding of their partners' feelings and experiences on a level that nonempaths will never get to endure.

Another gift that empaths sometimes have is that they can feel when someone or something is dangerous. Because empaths feel so deeply, it is common for them to pick up on a person's "bad" or "negative" energies or intent. This allows the empath to avoid possibly dangerous people and/or situations.

You may have experienced this. Can you remember a time when you have been in a group of people and gotten a "bad vibe" from someone in the group, but the rest of the party seemed to actually enjoy that person's company? Such an experience can certainly make you question your intuition. However, after some time has passed, maybe you learned something about the person that supported your initial intuition. The gift of feeling deeply can prevent you from entering dangerous situations, or getting too close to dangerous people.

Sensing Other People's Emotions

Being able to sense others' emotions has benefits, too. Many empathic people are virtually telepathic in nature. My client's husband, Travis, was annoyed, during the beginning of their relationship, that his wife could tell when something bothered him, even when he was attempting to avoid the topic. Now, however, he finds it very helpful when he walks in the door from work and she says, "Your vibe is different from usual. Would you like to talk?" For Travis, starting challenging and/or emotionally charged conversations is difficult. Now he loves that his wife can feel his energy, and if she asks if he would like to have a conversation it is a blessing to him.

I had a 15-year-old client tell me that she was once at the grocery store with her mother when suddenly she felt "taken over" by a sense of sadness and wanted to go hug a perfect stranger. She had the intuitive gift of clairempathy: She could feel the stranger's sadness. This wise girl knew that her ability to feel others' pain could be used to help. She rejoiced when sharing with me that by simply making eye contact and saying "hello" to a stranger at the grocery store, she could improve their mood, as well as her own!

KEY LESSONS AND REFLECTION

→ Being around people, especially in groups, must be balanced with alone time and self-care.

→ Setting boundaries starts with saying no, identifying your wants/needs, and asking for help.

→ Energy vampires and narcissists are especially draining for the empath. Avoid them if you can. If contact is inevitable, distance yourself, get a coach or therapist to help you, and/or use the gray rock method.

→ Smudging your home and cutting energetic cords are good ways to eliminate the toxicity from energy vampires and narcissists.

→ There are some great advantages of being able to feel and sense other people's emotions and/or vibes. It's helpful to remind yourself of these when you are feeling low.

Reflection Questions

1. What are some advantages that you have experienced in regard to feeling other people's emotions, energies, or vibes?

_____

_____

_____

_____

_____

2. Of the strategies in this chapter—Epsom and sea salt bath, binaural beats, eggshell/container visualization, cord cutting, smudging your space, narrative therapy, identifying your wants/needs, boundary setting, protecting yourself from energy vampires—which three were the most helpful? What was it about them that you liked?

_____

_____

_____

_____

3. How might you change or tweak any of the other exercises so that they might be more helpful to you?

_____

_____

_____

_____

_____

4. How can you put some of what you learned in chapter two into immediate action?

_____

_____

_____

_____

_____

CHAPTER 3

Empath Relationships

In chapter three we focus on some issues and challenges that empaths face in various types of relationships. Topics include dating, safe and unsafe people, identifying your relationship needs, codependency, toxic people, and long-term relationships. There is a quiz to help determine if you are in a codependent relationship and an exercise to assist you in determining who in your life is safe. There are also some great activities and exercises that will help you have the healthiest relationships possible.

DATING AS AN EMPATH

Empaths often struggle with the internal conflict of wanting to love and be loved, and the desire to be alone. Some empaths decide that romantic or intimate relationships are not something they want for themselves. This is perfectly normal for both empathic people and nonempaths. According to the Pew Research Center, 6 in 10 adults younger than 35 (60 percent) were living without a spouse or partner in 2017, up from 56 percent in 2007. Whether you are in a relationship, desire a relationship, or have decided against one, this chapter is for you.

Empaths may struggle with romantic relationships. These struggles may stem from being misunderstood by others. Empaths may scare potential partners because they will know and understand the people they date much faster than nonempathic daters. Additionally, empaths feel very deeply and have the need to be genuine and honest almost to a fault. These traits in combination can appear to others as too intense or moving too fast.

When dating, the empath often will be able to discern lies, no matter how big or small. Someone who dates an empath must be ready to be truthful, in all circumstances. Empaths appreciate honesty in a partner and feel betrayed when they are lied to.

Empaths make wonderful romantic partners. They are caring, thoughtful, and often romantic. They are good listeners, and will go out of their way to meet your wants and needs. They may be able to read you so well that you won't even have to say much: An empath who loves you may be able to understand what you are feeling/thinking, and just give you what you need without an exchange of words.

Empaths will feel with their partners. If you are angry, your empath partner will likely share that anger with you. Additionally, if you are excited about something, your empath partner will be as excited, and as you jump up and down together, you will experience why dating an empath is so wonderful.

Empaths feel more deeply than most, and this ability applies to positive emotions like joy, peace, excitement, appreciation, and amazement, as well as the experience of intense physical pleasure. Being with an empath can be the most pleasurable experience.

Identifying Your Relationship Needs

It is important for you to be able to identify your needs when it comes to a relationship. Not only will you be more adept at finding the right partner, but this understanding will also help you ask others to meet your relationship needs. Requesting that others meet their needs is very difficult for empathic people, but it is also important for them to practice. This exercise will help you identify your needs and practice asking for them to be met.

Using what you've learned about your empath experience so far from chapters one and two, including your answers to the exercises in those chapters, make a list of your personal empath traits, characteristics, and gifts.

EXAMPLE

YOUR EMPATH TRAIT	YOUR NEEDS IN A RELATIONSHIP
1. Needs alone time	*I need 30 minutes of alone time a day, even if I am living with a partner.*
2. Highly sensitive	*Because I can sense when someone is lying, I need my partner to be honest.*
3. Feels emotions and energies	*If I tell my partner that I need to leave a specific location or place with other people due to there being unpleasant energy, I need them to respect that.*

YOUR EMPATH TRAIT	YOUR NEEDS IN A RELATIONSHIP
1.	
2.	
3.	
4.	
5.	
6.	
7.	
8.	
9.	
10.	

Asking Others for What You Need

Whether you are dating, single, or in a committed relationship, asking others to meet your needs is important. Once you are able to identify your needs, big or small, you can practice telling others what they are.

In the previous exercise, you identified some of your needs. Now you'll write out a request that honors each need. Here is an example:

My need: I need 30 minutes of alone time a day, even if I am living with a partner.

Put into a request: My job requires that I interact with people all day, so I really need to have 30 minutes each evening to myself. Could you ask me each day when I would like to take that alone time?

1. **My need:**

_____

_____

   Put into a request:

_____

_____

2. **My need:**

_____

_____

   Put into a request:

_____

_____

3. My need:

_____

_____

Put into a request:

_____

_____

4. My need:

_____

_____

Put into a request:

_____

_____

5. My need:

_____

_____

Put into a request:

_____

_____

6. My need:

_____

_____

Put into a request:

_____

_____

7. My need:

_____

_____

Put into a request:

_____

_____

8. My need:

_____

_____

Put into a request:

_____

_____

9. My need:

_____

_____

Put into a request:

_____

_____

10. My need:

_____

_____

Put into a request:

_____

_____

Again, feel free to continue this exercise on a separate sheet of paper if you like.

LONG-TERM RELATIONSHIPS

The closer an empath grows to someone, the more sensitive they are to their emotions, energies, and thoughts. Long-term relationships, then, can be a source of both great joy and immense stress. Empaths often feel drained by the additional stimulation that accompanies relationships. Sometimes empaths develop maladaptive patterns in regard to relationships in an attempt to protect themselves from the overwhelm that can occur in relationships.

Some empaths will be attracted to emotionally unavailable partners. One of my clients was a good-looking, successful, and kind man in his late 40s. He repeatedly dated, and married, shallow and vapid women. Initially, he believed that he was tricked by these women, and that he had no way of knowing that they were emotionally unavailable until after he married them. As we explored, however, he discovered that he was actually seeking women with very little emotional capacity. He came to realize that he was doing this because he knew that he could not become overwhelmed by the women's emotions. He desperately wanted to find his soul mate, but his intense fear of becoming overwhelmed in an emotionally intimate relationship kept his dream of a fulfilling relationship out of reach.

When empathic people have relationships with emotionally available partners, the amount of joy, happiness, and delight is unrivaled. When the empath and their partner are emotionally healthy, the union can be astonishing. The connection between empaths and their partners is so powerful that strangers will often comment on the couple's interactions. An emotionally available partner who recognizes the empath's intuitive gifts and deep sensitivities is irreplaceable. When the partner of an empath recognizes these sensitivities and gifts, the empath is validated and empowered. This is an incredible experience for the empath, which will make the empath want to cherish and treat the partner well.

When two empaths are romantically involved, the experience can be extraordinary. The pair may experience the relationship as two halves coming together for the first time. They may refer to themselves as soul mates or twin flames. The communication between two empath lovers can be unparalleled. No words are spoken, yet the pair understands and responds appropriately to each other. The sex life of an empath couple is incredible because they sense what their partner likes and dislikes, and respond fittingly.

Six Tips for Maintaining Healthy Relationships

Here are six tips to keep your cool while in a romantic relationship. Under each tip, answer the question on a scale of 1 to 10 (1 being rarely and 10 being often).

1. **Do not take things personally.** It is inevitable that your partner will critique something you do. Be mindful of your interpretation, and try not to take it to heart. React or respond in a loving and nondefensive manner.

   On the 1–10 rating scale, how often do you not take things personally? Where on the scale would you *like* to be? What is one step you can take toward the score you would like to have?

   _____

   _____

2. **Stop trying to fix your partner.** We can't "fix" other people, or force someone to change. The most likely result is you feeling frustrated, and your partner feeling critiqued.

   Using the 1–10 scale, how often have you tried to "fix" a romantic partner? Where on the scale would you *like* to be? What is one step you can take toward the score you would like to have?

   _____

   _____

3. **Do not yell or name-call.** Empaths are sensitive to disagreements to begin with. If voices get raised, you may feel so drained at the end of it all, that it takes days to recover. Name-calling has a similar effect. It will hurt your partner, and drain the empath.

   Using the 1–10 scale, how often have you called a romantic partner a name, or raised your voice? Where on the scale would you *like* to be? What is one step you can take toward the score you would like to have?

   _____

   _____

4. **Take daily alone time.** Even if you love nothing more than time with your partner, you need to set aside some alone time each and every day. This time will help you feel replenished, and will allow you to have more to give, resulting in you being a better partner yourself.

    Using the 1–10 scale, how often do you take alone time? Where on the scale would you *like* to be? What is one step you can take toward the score you would like to have?

    _____

    _____

5. **Regulate the sound in your home.** Empathic people are generally quiet, and feel their best when their environments are quiet. Loud music, blaring TVs, or multiple competing sounds will drive an empath crazy very quickly. Have a discussion with your partner about sound. Come to an agreement on what sounds are acceptable, and at what times of day they are prohibited.

    Using the 1–10 scale, how often do you communicate to your partner (or past partners) your needs around the sounds in your home? Where on the scale would you *like* to be? What is one step you can take toward the score you would like to have?

    _____

    _____

6. **Engage in play.** Empaths tend to be serious much of the time, so play of some sort is important for balance. Play with your partner by doing art, going geocaching, or engaging in an activity that makes you both laugh like schoolchildren.

    Using the 1–10 scale, how often do you play with your partner (or past partners)? Where on the scale would you *like* to be? What is one step you can take toward the score you would like to have?

    _____

    _____

Relationship Reflection

Take some time to think about the following questions. Write down your answers, and if you are feeling brave and are currently in a relationship, share them with your partner.

1. What brought you and your partner together? Is that the same thing that keeps you together now?

_____

_____

2. If your partner could live inside your brain/body for a month, what about you do you think they would be surprised by?

_____

_____

3. What are three things that you would like your partner to better understand about you?

_____

_____

_____

4. With your relationship in mind, what are the benefits of partnering with another empath?

_____

_____

5. With your relationship in mind, what are the most challenging aspects of partnering with another empath?

_____

_____

DEEPER PRACTICE:
RELATIONSHIP VALUES EXERCISE

If you are single, complete part A. If you are part of a couple, complete parts A, B, and C.

A. On the next page is a list that contains various values that pertain to romantic relationships. Write each one separately on slips of paper. Then, sort the papers into three categories:

    1. Extremely important to have in a relationship

    2. Somewhat important to have in a relationship

    3. Not important to have in a relationship

Once you have them sorted into three piles, narrow down the "extremely important" cards to your top 10.

B. After you have identified your most important 10 cards, ask your partner to do the card sort. It is important that you do not share your top 10 with your partner until you have both chosen your final 10 cards.

C. Once both your partner and you have completed the card sort, compare your top 10 values. Answer the following questions:

    1. How many of the 10 did you and your partner both have in common?

    _____

    2. Were you surprised by any of your partner's cards? If so, talk (or write) about why you were surprised.

    _____

    _____

    3. In your 10 cards, are there any values that are nonnegotiable? If so, did your partner also have this value in their top 10 list?

    _____

    _____

4. If, in number 3, your nonnegotiable value(s) were not on your partner's top 10 list, what does that mean to you? Does that impact the future of your relationship?

    _____

    _____

5. What is the biggest lesson that you and your partner can take from this experience?

    _____

    _____

Acceptance	Exploration	Impact	Power
Admiration	Faithfulness	Industry	Responsibility
Adventure	Fame	Intimacy	Risk Taking
Advocacy	Family	Justice	Safety
Autonomy	Fitness	Knowledge	Self-control
Challenge	Forgiveness	Learning	Self-esteem
Comfort	Friendship	Legacy	Service
Commitment	Fun	Leisure	Sexuality
Compassion	Genuineness	Love	Solitude
Confidence	God's will	Mindfulness	Spirituality
Conformity	Gratitude	Monogamy	Status
Contribution	Growth	Notoriety	Superiority
Control	Health	Ownership	Tradition
Courtesy	Hobbies	Passion	Wealth
Creativity	Hope	Peace	
Dependability	Humility	Pleasure	
Enlightenment	Humor	Popularity	

CODEPENDENCY

The term *codependent* originated as a way to describe a person who had a romantic relationship with an alcoholic and who demonstrated the need for that alcoholic partner to remain "sick." "Codependent" has become broader and now describes people who enable their partner's addiction, poor mental health, irresponsibility, immaturity, or other unhealthy behavior. Codependency negatively affects your ability to have a healthy and fulfilling partnership, due to its one-sided nature.

Empaths can be codependents, and some empath traits can appear as though they are codependent characteristics. Both the empath and the codependent sometimes have issues with regulating their emotions. The codependent will go into "fixer" mode quickly when someone asks for their support because they cannot tolerate the other person's emotional discomfort. The empath, on the other hand, is able to hold space for others who come to them for support. By listening and allowing the emotions of another to be what they are, they offer validation, even resolution.

The codependent has diffuse boundaries with others, and seeks to caretake, often to their own detriment. It is true that the untrained empath may similarly sacrifice their own needs for the well-being of others. This self-sacrifice comes about for different reasons, however. The codependent person caretakes in an attempt to avoid being uncomfortable with other people's negative moods. The empath's reason for self-sacrifice is usually more about a genuine desire to help and care for others.

Empathy is different from codependency in a multitude of ways. Healthy or empowered empaths have a solid sense of self. We understand that we do not need to own, or take personally, the emotional states and/or behavior of others. We know that other people's emotions are not our responsibility to change, or fix. Conversely, the codependent individual feels responsible for, and will attempt to change, other people's emotions and behaviors. The empath's stable sense of self allows them to remember that how other people respond to them is purely about that person, and not an indication of who *they* are. A codependent person is likely to let their sense of self be dictated by the opinions of others.

Let's use Maria and Jada as an example to demonstrate the difference between an empath and a codependent. The couple is at Maria's parents' home, celebrating Thanksgiving. Jada is uneasy being there because Maria's family is not comfortable with lesbian relationships. Jada attempts to cope with her feelings by making inappropriate jokes at Maria's family's expense. Everyone at the dinner table becomes troubled, tense, and quiet.

If Maria were codependent, she would likely ignore Jada's making fun of the family, in an attempt to avoid conflict with her partner. She may even excuse Jada's behavior by saying that it was Jada's way of dealing with an uncomfortable family gathering. If Maria was an empath, and not codependent, things would be much different. She would address Jada's behavior, either as it occurred or after the gathering. She would not make excuses for Jada's behavior, and she would ask that Jada not make the same mistake again.

It can be challenging for empaths to avoid codependent behavior, because they are so tuned in to the feelings of others. It is important for empaths to be aware of what codependent behavior is, and to have insight into their own wants and needs to avoid such behavior. Empaths frequently put others' needs ahead of their own, which is also a trait of a codependent person. Empaths who prioritize their own well-being feel better, and have more to offer their loved ones at the end of the day.

Are You Codependent?

This quiz will help you see whether you have codependent tendencies. Circle yes or no in response to each question.

1. Do you give until you are completely depleted?   Yes   No
2. Does the idea of abandonment make you upset?   Yes   No
3. Do you typically defer to others to make decisions, or do you second-guess your decisions?   Yes   No
4. When in relationships, do you focus more on your partner's happiness than your own?   Yes   No
5. Do you feel guilty for saying no?   Yes   No
6. Do you often feel like you need to "rescue" others, or fix their problems for them?   Yes   No
7. Do you sometimes allow others to act selfishly in order to avoid a fight?   Yes   No
8. Are other people's opinions of you extremely important to you?   Yes   No
9. Is it hard for you to set boundaries with others?   Yes   No
10. Have you ever had to take time off from work because of a relationship in your life?   Yes   No
11. Do you tend to hang on to relationships as long as possible? Even if friends say you should leave?   Yes   No

If you answered yes to six or more of these questions, you may be codependent. See the Resources to find out more about this important topic.

Strategies for Empaths to Avoid Codependent Tendencies

1. **Stop trying to "save" other people.** Empaths naturally try to ease any pain of the people around them. This becomes codependent behavior when they try to "save" a person, "fix" a person, or when easing another's pain comes at a cost to their own well-being.

    What could you do instead of saving or fixing a friend who comes to you for help?

    ---

2. **Stop avoiding confrontation and/or difficult conversations.** Avoidance of difficult conversations and/or arguments with your partner is a sign that you are in a codependent relationship. Rather than avoiding, practice having such discussions in a healthy, respectful manner.

    Who in your life do you need to have a difficult conversation with? What is an assertive and healthy way for you to start that conversation?

    ---

3. **Identify your needs.** We cannot meet our needs, nor can we ask others to meet our needs, if we are unaware of what they are. Empaths often find this difficult, as they are so focused on other people's needs and desires.

    If you had 30 days with no contact with others, which of your needs would you make a priority?

    ---

4. **Ask for your needs to be met.** Empaths often expect people to know what they need, but nonempaths do not have this ability. You must ask for what you need in a clear and concise manner.

   What is one thing that you could request from someone, in regard to your needs? Ideas: a birthday party, a hug, time alone, a specific gift, help with a chore.

   _____

   _____

5. **Continually work on healthy boundaries.** The healthier your boundaries are, the less you will feel drained and/or overwhelmed.

   If you could easily keep one boundary, which one would you choose, and why? For example, saying no, asking for your needs to be met, boundaries around time or noise, or sexual boundaries.

   _____

   _____

   _____

6. **Be aware of your self-worth.** You are just as important and worthy as anyone else. Developing self-worth will allow you to enforce healthy boundaries.

   Name two strategies that you are willing to utilize that would help develop your sense of self-worth.

   _____

   _____

NAVIGATING FRIENDSHIPS

Empaths are typically introverted, so the idea of maintaining friendships can feel daunting. There are some challenges that empaths face when preserving friendships. Obviously, to have friends, one must have some amount of social interaction, which can be draining for many empaths. Having friends also means that the empath will receive more invitations to large social gatherings, which are often overwhelming. Additionally, when an empath feels connected to a friend, they will feel that friend's emotions so strongly that it is hard to separate from them.

Having a couple of close friends is important for the empath, however. Luckily, empaths tend to make friends easily, and keep these friends for long periods of time. Having close friendships allows the empath to see life with more meaning. Friends will encourage and support the empath, helping them to see the best parts of themselves even in dark times. Friends will also help validate the empath and their intuitive abilities, which is advantageous to all empaths. Healthy friendships foster a give-and-take relationship, so the empath is able to ask for help, and may even gain energy from close friends.

A Closer Look at Relationships

1. Think of the various relationships you have with people. Write each person's name in the bull's-eye below. People you identify as "safe" are placed in the center of the bull's-eye. "Questionable" people go in the middle ring, and "unsafe" people in the outer ring. Make sure to include at least 10 people somewhere on the bull's-eye before moving on to step 2.

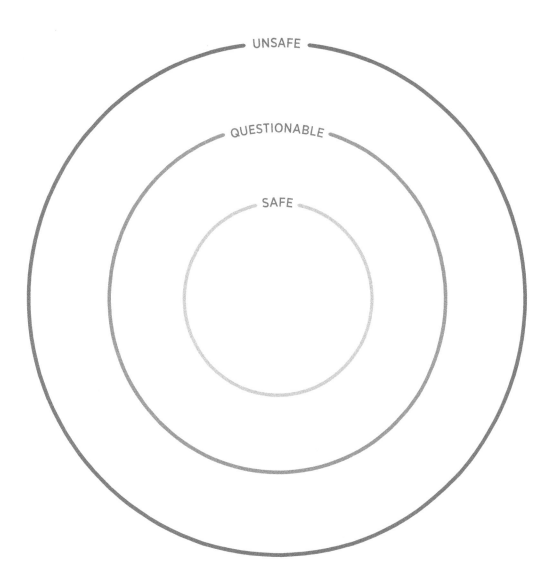

2. Next, let's take a closer look at what constitutes a "safe," "questionable," and "unsafe" person.

Safe: A safe person is someone who has earned your trust through multiple positive experiences. They have kept personal information about you private, have done what they said they would do, are reliable, and have your best interests in mind. People in the "safe" group have never deliberately hurt you. If they have hurt you accidentally, they have apologized and made it right with you. Typically, my clients only have one to four individuals in the "safe" group.

Questionable: If you suspect that someone has malevolent intentions, they might be in this (or the "unsafe") category. People who avoid taking responsibility, or who are self-righteous, could also fall into either the "questionable" or "unsafe" categories, depending on how their behavior affects you. Additionally, defensive or negative individuals could land here or in "unsafe," depending on their effect on you and how extreme these traits are. If you are not 100 percent certain that a friend belongs in the "safe" category, then they should be placed in the "questionable" category until you are absolutely certain they are safe in all regards. The "questionable" category will likely have the highest number of individuals.

Unsafe: People in this category are here either because they have deliberately hurt you, they caused a minor hurt and did not apologize, or simply because you suspect they have malicious intentions. Empaths often put strangers into the "questionable" category. However, I encourage my clients not to do this. The very nature of a stranger means that you have no way of knowing if they are dangerous or not. Thus, more often than not, strangers should be placed in the "unsafe" category.

Having read the descriptions above, would you change where you placed people within the first bull's-eye? Take some time to think about each individual in the bull's-eye, and place them in the second bull's-eye (opposite), where you think they are best categorized. Then answer the questions that follow.

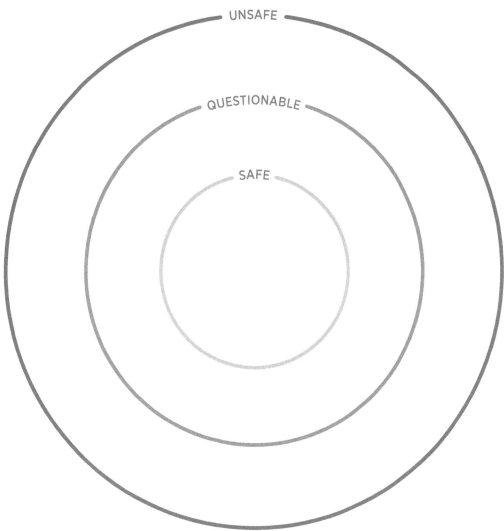

UNSAFE

QUESTIONABLE

SAFE

1. What made you move the people from one category to another?

_____

_____

_____

2. How would you know when it was okay for you to move someone from the "questionable" category to the "safe" category?

_____

_____

_____

3. How many people do you believe you should have in the "safe" category, and why?

_____

_____

4. Where would you place a parent, if they were sometimes emotionally manipulative?

_____

5. What might someone have to do for you to push them from "safe" to "questionable"?

_____

_____

6. What might someone have to do for you to push them from "questionable" to "unsafe"?

_____

_____

7. Does this change how you might interact with anyone in your day-to-day life? If so, how should it change to be healthy for you?

_____

_____

EMPATHS AND TOXIC FRIENDSHIPS

Because empaths are frequently labeled as "too sensitive," we sometimes attempt to hide our sensitivities under the guise of independence. We also commonly seek self-validation for our sensitivities, which draws us to people who need help or a lot of attention. We seem to have an affinity toward keeping wounded and unhealthy people in our circle of friends. It can sometimes feel more comfortable for the empath to allow a friend to do all of the talking, because it protects us from vulnerability and judgment. Healthy friendship requires two people to both be vulnerable, and to show mutual respect for each other. There should be an even exchange of give-and-take in healthy friendships, and often this is missing in the friendships that empaths keep.

An empath's affinity for trying to heal others can sometimes create unbalanced, even codependent friendships. This kind of unbalanced friendship will ultimately lead to the empath feeling drained, even feeling used and resentful. Furthermore, emotional vampires tend to seek friendship specifically with empathic people, and seem to have a good radar for who we are. As empaths we absorb this friend's emotions. Although this provides the energy vampire relief, it is exhausting and depleting for the empath. These types of friendships eventually wear the empath so thin, that the friendship ends.

It is important for the empath to surround themselves with friends who are healthy, generally happy, and who participate fully in a reciprocal relationship. An empath with a healthy group of friends will be much more likely to stay grounded. Healthy friends give and receive love, acceptance, and emotional support, all of which are necessary for the empath to live their best life.

Toxic versus Healthy Friendships: A Checklist

Think about a friend who has elicited negative emotions in you. This can be a person you are currently friends with or someone from your past. Take a look at the lists below, and circle each item that is true for that friend. For example, if the friend is trustworthy, but is sometimes passive-aggressive, circle both "trustworthy," in the "signs of a healthy friend" category, and "passive-aggressive" in the "signs of a toxic friend" category.

SIGNS OF A HEALTHY FRIEND	SIGNS OF A TOXIC FRIEND
Good listener	Does all the talking, all the time
Calls to make plans	Calls only if needing something
Supportive of you	Competitive with you
Excited for your successes	Jealous of your successes
Asks for reasonable things	Asks for things you cannot provide
Energizes or inspires you	Drains you
Respects your boundaries	Pushes or ignores your boundaries
Works through conflict with you	Blames you for all conflict
Assertive yet kind	Passive-aggressive or aggressive
Flexible	Controlling
Trustworthy	Deceitful

Now count the number of qualities you circled in each category. If the friend has significantly more qualities of a healthy friend, that is a good indicator that the friend is healthy. If the friend has more qualities in the "signs of a toxic friend" category, you may want to reconsider the friendship.

Of course, every person has flaws, but the characteristics in the "toxic" category are ones that stretch beyond a flaw and into toxic behavior. Take a moment to consider all of the traits that you circled and answer the following questions:

1. Is this a friend you want to continue to spend time with? Why or why not?

_____

_____

_____

2. In regard to this friend, did you circle any traits in the "signs of a toxic friend" category? How many did you circle? What does this say about your friendship?

_____

_____

_____

3. If you have a friend with one or more traits in the "toxic" category, would it be worth your time to discuss this with your friend? Why or why not?

_____

_____

_____

4. If you have found that your friend has some toxic traits and you think it might be healthy for you to either end the friendship or distance yourself from the friend, how might you go about this?

_____

_____

_____

DEEPER PRACTICE:
THE HO'OPONOPONO MANTRA

The Hawaiian word *ho'oponopono* comes from *ho'o* ("to make") and *pono* ("right"). The ho'oponopono prayer, or mantra, is one that is used to heal from relationships that are, or have been, toxic. This does not mean that you have to resume the friendship with the person. Instead, you heal the rift in the relationship, and in doing so you set yourself free from the energetic connection to that person. The ho'oponopono mantra translates to "I love you, I am sorry, please forgive me." The idea is that when you get right with other people, you become right with yourself.

In the book *Zero Limits: The Secret Hawaiian System for Wealth, Health, Peace, and More*, authors Joe Vitale and Ihaleakala Hew Len, PhD, a master of modern ho'oponopono teachings, explain that we are responsible for everything in our lives. Even if you had nothing to do with a situation, you are responsible for it because you manifested it into your world. This is a core concept of the ho'oponopono practice.

How to Use the Ho'oponopono Mantra

1. First, meditate on the feeling you wish to have when the energetic connection between you and the identified person is gone. The feeling may be peace, forgiveness, love, separation, or any feeling that resonates with you.
2. Now that you have the emotion in mind, recount how you and this person ended up where you are now. For example: What was said, done, or felt that was harmful?
3. Consciously release all that caused the harm. Then, begin chanting the ho'oponopono mantra aloud:

I Love You,
I'm Sorry,
Please Forgive Me,
Thank You.

4. Repeat it as many times as you feel necessary to eradicate the energetic connection between you and this person. I recommend repeating it at least 20 times. You may feel the desire to practice this mantra for several days in a row to fully alleviate the connection.

KEY LESSONS AND REFLECTION

→ Many people, both empaths and nonempaths, decide not to have romantic relationships.

→ *Codependency* is a term that describes someone who enables their partner's unhealthy and damaging behavior.

→ Some traits of empathic people can appear to be codependent traits.

→ Good ways to avoid codependent behavior include identifying your needs, asking for your needs to be met, not avoiding conflict, working on healthy boundaries, and developing positive self-esteem.

→ Knowing your values is helpful when identifying what your boundaries should be.

Reflection Questions

1. What are some of your most important needs in a romantic relationship?

_____

_____

_____

_____

_____

2. How might you ask someone for your needs to be met?

_____

_____

_____

_____

_____

3. What are your nonnegotiable values in relationships?

_____

_____

_____

_____

4. Do you (or your partner) have any codependent tendencies? If so, what are they?

_____

_____

_____

_____

5. Do you currently have any toxic friends? If so, what do you plan to do, moving forward?

_____

_____

_____

_____

6. What constitutes whether someone is "safe," "questionable," or "unsafe"?

_____

_____

_____

_____

CHAPTER 4

The Empath Family

Navigating relationships with family members can be a challenge for many empaths. But empaths can benefit greatly from family relationships, too.

In this chapter we'll explore how to handle the strong emotional responses we often feel when we're interacting with our families. It will also help you identify ways you like to receive love and discuss how understanding your unique ways of loving others and receiving love sustains all relationships.

Additionally, we'll discuss parenting, including how to deal with your child's emotions, your parenting stress, and the joys and challenges of raising an empath child. The techniques and exercises in this chapter will help you feel your best as you navigate family relationships of all kinds.

FAMILY LIFE

Families can elicit a variety of strong emotional responses, both positive and negative, for empaths. Often our parents, siblings, spouses, and children know us so well that they have the ability to hurt us like nobody else. They can bring up the past in ways that can reinjure us, as well.

Most empathic people do not go around telling everyone that they are an empath, much less share the details of what that entails. Thus, having family that understands the empath is extremely beneficial because it provides validity to who they are, as well as to the way they experience the world.

For example, one of the reasons I adore my relationship with my mother is the fact that I can simply say "My ears," and she turns off the TV and drastically lowers her voice. I cannot imagine anyone but family honoring my sensitive hearing in this way.

Gratitude Journaling

Robert Emmons, PhD, the leading expert on gratitude, has published numerous studies demonstrating the benefits of gratitude. Any form of gratitude practice seems to increase happiness; improve physical health, sleep, and self-esteem; and improve interpersonal relationships.

Practicing gratitude moves your attention away from negative emotions, such as resentment and anger. Through practicing gratitude, we become more in touch with the ways we have been supported and cared for by our family and friends. Empaths who practice gratitude may experience more positive or pleasant emotions when thinking about family members.

Think about a family member who elicits in you some mild negative emotions. These feelings may be annoyance, envy, or competition. Each day for the next two weeks, take 10 minutes to write down all the reasons you can think of to be grateful for this person. Anything goes here, big or small. Maybe your brother watched your dog while you were on a vacation in 1999, or maybe your mother gave you $10,000 to put down on your first home.

Start practicing gratitude now, and write down your first "Gratitude Journal" entry here:

_____

_____

_____

_____

_____

_____

_____

_____

_____

_____

_____

_____

_____

MAKING LOVING REQUESTS

Empaths will often prioritize people they love, above all else. I had a client, Tameka, who had been married to her husband, Jed, for 10 years. She was very good at fore-seeing what he wanted and needed. She knew, for instance, that after a long workday, he enjoyed a warm meal while reading the sports section of the paper. So she would cook and open the paper to the sports section for him when he returned from work. She could also tell when Jed was upset or trying to work something out in his head, and she would always respond in a loving way.

Tameka came to me because she was ready to leave Jed. She was exasperated that although she had been anticipating and meeting his needs for years, he seemed oblivious to her desires. She cried in my office as she described Jed taking a phone call while she was mid-sentence with him. At the movies, he would read his text messages or fall asleep, which did not allow for any conversation about the film afterward.

The last straw for Tameka was when they took a five-day trip to Mexico, where Jed spent most of his time on work calls or talking to strangers in the lobby. Tameka felt like Jed's last priority, and she felt abandoned, as he seemed to disappear for hours while on this vacation.

Tameka's story illustrates a common occurrence for empathic people: Although they understand their loved ones' emotions and are great at predicting what their family's needs are, they are not met with the same consideration.

This lack of reciprocity is, however, not always the fault of our family members. Because empaths are born with their intuitive gifts in tow, many of us forget that we are the minority. We forget that other people are unable to feel our emotions and thus are not able to identify our needs unless we express them. The vast majority of my empath clients have to learn to be assertive with regard to their emotions, wants, and needs. We must express our emotions, and communicate what we want and need, rather than expecting our loved ones to "just know" like we do.

Tameka decided that she would try being more assertive with Jed. One thing she did was explain to him that when he takes phone calls during their conversations, it makes her feel sad and unloved. She then asked him to change that behavior. With tears in his eyes, he apologized to her. He agreed to change, and to this day, the couple is happily married.

Requesting specific loving actions from your loved ones comes with an added bonus: If you have empathic children, you're modeling how to communicate lovingly with nonempaths and how to set healthy boundaries.

An Empath's Love Letter to Their Family: How to Score Love Points with Me

This exercise will help you put into words the kinds of loving actions you'd like to receive from your loved ones.

Fill in the blanks to the following statements. Add any additional sentences that pertain to your emotions, wants, and needs.

→ I really, really love it when you _____.

→ To me, a picture-perfect evening with you would look like this: _____

_____.

→ When I've had a difficult day, the best thing you can do for me is _____

_____.

→ Of all the things you do for me, the things I value the most are _____

_____.

→ Without _____, I'd be absolutely miserable.

→ When you do/say _____, I know you love me.

→ I feel safe, valued, and loved when you _____.

EMPATH PARENTING

Empaths who choose to have children of their own; coparent their partners' children; or maintain close relationships with the children of family members or friends can develop an incredible connection with these youngsters. Additionally, the awareness of the challenges of being an empath and having a parental role may result in some empaths deciding not to have children, and that is perfectly normal as well.

Because empathic people are naturally kind, giving, and nurturing, they make excellent parents and caregivers. The intuitive abilities of the empath allow for a proactive approach to parenting, as they sense things in their children that most non-empaths cannot. Often, empathic parents experience spiritual lessons and exponential growth as a result of parenting or caring for children.

Dealing with Your Child's Emotions

As an empathic parent or caregiver, you are capable of feeling everything a child feels. Sometimes it's difficult to separate a child's emotions from your own. Because many empath parents and caregivers experience a connection with their child that is inexplicably deep, it is important to practice separating your emotions from your child's emotions. Doing so will help you stay centered and provide your children with a role model for healthy behavior.

Empath Parenting

Take a few minutes in a quiet and comfortable place to think about the challenges that you have encountered while dealing with your child's emotions and/or struggles. Answer the following:

1. Have you experienced any *themes* in regard to your challenges as an empath parent? If so, what are those themes? (Some examples: You struggle emotionally every time your child is in physical pain. You suffer from insomnia when your child is away from home. You constantly experience overwhelm when your child cries.)

    _____

    _____

    _____

2. What would help you overcome the struggles that seem to come up repeatedly? Answer this with no limitations in mind. For example, answer as though you have unlimited money, social support, or time.

    _____

    _____

    _____

3. What people and resources (that you have not yet tried) might be available to assist you with overcoming these obstacles?

_____

_____

4. Set a goal to check into these possibilities by a certain date, or within a certain amount of time. Write that goal here:

_____

_____

5. What are some of the benefits of being an empath parent?

_____

_____

_____

Tapping with Your Empath Child

Tapping is a technique that combines ancient Chinese acupressure and modern psychology to physically adjust your brain, body, and emotional energy simultaneously. It consists of tapping on specific points on your body with your fingers. These points are located along meridians, or energy pathways, that run through the body. The tapping on these points sends signals to the amygdala. This part of the brain is sometimes referred to as the "fear center" of the brain, as the "fight or flight" response is initiated here. The amygdala is not controlled by the frontal lobe, meaning that logic and thinking do not control it.

9. TOP OF HEAD

2. EYEBROW

3. SIDE OF EYE

4. UNDER EYE

5. UNDER NOSE

6. CHIN

7. COLLARBONE

8. UNDER ARM

1. KARATE CHOP

Tapping while concentrating on alleviating a negative emotion restores your body and emotional state to homeostasis, and you should feel relief from the negative emotion quickly.

This is a great technique to teach to or practice with an empath child. They can easily remember how to do it. And it does not require the use of any tools, so it can be done anywhere.

1. To start, have your child identify what they are feeling.

    It often helps to have your child look at a chart with pictures of people showing different emotions. (See the Resources section for one source for feelings charts.)

    Write down what your child is feeling on the line below, and if they are old enough to do so, have them rate its intensity on a scale of 1 to 10 (1 being very low and 10 being very high).

    Ask your child to pay attention to the feeling while they do step 2.

2. Using your fingertips to tap on your own body, show your child how to tap on each of the meridian points shown in the illustration (opposite). Tap on the points in the numbered order (starting with Karate Chop), and tap on each point eight times before moving on to the next point.

3. After your child does one round of tapping, ask them to rate the intensity of their negative emotion again. Write the intensity on the line below.

_____

4. If the intensity of your child's emotion is a 3 or higher, or if they still appear distressed, have your child tap on the points again. Repeat the tapping technique as many times as it takes to significantly lower the intensity of your child's negative emotion to a 2 or under.

Tip: You can also use tapping yourself to address negative emotions or reduce parenting/family stress.

Dealing with Your Own Stress

Parenting can be stressful and draining, especially for empath parents. It is imperative, then, that empath parents make self-care and stress management a priority. Attempting to parent while exhausted only pushes the empath toward mental health issues like depression, and/or toward the use of unhealthy coping tools such as drinking and drug use.

Visualizing Parenting Joy

Here's a short visualization-based practice you can do in the evening or in the morning, when your children are asleep, to help yourself feel calm, relaxed, and more positive about parenting.

1. Find a quiet, comfortable place to sit. Settle in and take five deep breaths.
2. Give yourself permission to relax your muscles. Take five more deep breaths, paying close attention to your muscles as they let go, unwind, and relax. Work from your face down your neck and back, down your legs, and into your feet.
3. Give yourself permission to let go of worries, any to-do lists, or other people's energy. Then imagine yourself surrounded by a white light. Take a few more deep breaths.
4. Now take some time to appreciate the joys of being a parent. This may include watching, in your mind's eye, your child as they explore and get excited at every new experience . . . or you think about how strong you are, as you do any- and everything to protect them as they grow and test boundaries. Maybe you focus on the amount of love you feel for your child—love in such amounts you could never have imagined it until you held your child in your arms for the first time.
5. Take a few more deep breaths and allow yourself to feel relaxed, free of worry, and filled with some of the joy that being a parent has brought you.

Energy Healing for the Empath

Any hands-on or body-movement technique that helps your natural energy to flow with ease throughout your body is a type of *energy healing* or *energy medicine*. You likely already use energy healing techniques without even realizing you are doing so. Some examples are rocking your body, rubbing your body, stretching, and taking a deep breath.

Below are three simple but effective energy healing techniques to try when you're feeling stressed.

→ Put your hand on your forehead and leave it there for 2 to 3 minutes. When you get stressed, you lose blood from your forebrain because it goes into your body for the fight-or-flight response. Because your hand is electromagnetic, as is your blood, putting your hand on your forehead for a couple of minutes draws the blood back up into your brain. This technique is good for alleviating stress and anxiety because it interrupts the fight-or-flight response.

→ Stand up in a space where you have room to move your body freely. Begin by lifting one knee, setting it down, and lifting your other knee. It should feel like you are walking in place. Continue this movement and add your arms by swinging them in an exaggerated way. Again, it will feel as though you are walking in place but exaggerating the movements. This movement allows the energy in your body to move freely and to connect across both sides of your body. Do this 25 times.

→ Place your hands on your head, with your fingers in a curled position, and with your pinky fingers at the hairline. Now push into your head gently, then pull your hands away from each other as you do so. You will pull down and out about 3 to 4 inches. Now move your hands (in the same position) back a few inches, behind where you just pulled. Again, push into your head gently, then pull out a few inches. You will end when your hands are positioned at the top, back of your head. If this felt especially pleasant, repeat as many times as you like. This is great for releasing any energy that is "stuck." It also releases tension in the skin and muscles on your head, which allows you to pull more cerebrospinal fluid into the brain. (This happens naturally in us when we are not tense or overwhelmed.) I find this most helpful after working on the computer.

These three techniques come from Donna Eden, a pioneer in the field of energy medicine. For more on her work, including more of her techniques, see the Resources section at the end of this workbook.

1. Which of these energy techniques did you like best, and why?

_____

_____

2. Commit to using your favorite technique when you are feeling stressed. Write some sort of a reminder on a sticky note and put it in a place where you will see it frequently.

DEEPER PRACTICE: CRYSTALS, ROCKS, AND GEMS, OH MY!

The use of crystals and rocks to regulate your mood can be extremely helpful. As an empath coach, I keep quartz crystal throughout my office—under the couch, in all four corners of my room, on my desk. I also keep them in my home. Quartz is known as the "master healer" of stones and gems. It is said to amplify your energy and can also increase the intensity from other stones. It absorbs, stores, and regulates energy.

Clear quartz crystal specifically is known for its ability to clear the mind of negativity, to enhance personal awareness and growth, and to act as a beacon of light.

Quartz crystals also maintain a very precise frequency. They can be programmed to hold certain frequencies, so quartz is often used in radios, micro compressors, and many other tech-related applications. Watchmakers use it to keep timepieces accurate due to its ability to hold a certain frequency.

I also keep black tourmaline in my office to help my clients regulate mood. Black tourmaline is said to be a protective stone that repels and removes negative energies from a person or a space. This rock is wonderful for grounding when you are feeling overwhelmed. It also balances and harmonizes all of the chakras.

At home, I keep black tourmaline in my bedroom near my cell phone. Research shows that black tourmaline is the best stone to use against harmful electromagnetic fields, including the ones from your computer and cell phone.

My Top 10 Crystals for Empaths

Amethyst—My very favorite crystal because it aids in the development of the empath's intuitive gifts.

Aqua aura quartz—This crystal provides protection from harmful energies, whether trapped inside or coming from external sources.

Black obsidian—If you need extremely powerful protection, black obsidian is my go-to. Be careful, however, because it can bring you into an emotional low if you are not in dire need of protection.

Black tourmaline—This crystal is great for transmuting energy. It is very calming, and will reduce anxiety when you hold it in your hands.

Clear quartz—Known as the "master healer," clear quartz amplifies positive energy and absorbs and stores negative energy. You can program it to hold any intention of your choosing.

Lodestone—Because of its magnetic properties, this stone will balance the polarities within your electromagnetic field. It is also said to help alleviate the feelings of overwhelm that empaths often experience.

Purple jade—This gem is associated with the earth star chakra, which is about six inches below our feet. Having purple jade near you assists in keeping you grounded. It is also considered a powerful protective stone for empaths.

Rose quartz—The stone of universal love. Rose quartz is supportive of unconditional love, and it restores harmony in romantic relationships. This crystal also aids in comfort during times of grief.

Smoky quartz—This crystal also transmutes negative energy, and is said to detoxify your environment. If it looks almost black, chances are it's irradiated. Yeah, it's giving off radiation. Get out your Geiger counter, and stay away from it.

Sugilite—This crystal provides an energetic field of protection around you, shielding you from other people's energy. It also helps balance your electromagnetic field.

PARENTING AN EMPATH CHILD

Parenting an empath child can be full of wonderful experiences, and it also has unique challenges.

Teaching your empath child to cherish their intuition and trust their gut feelings allows the child to develop their gifts in valuable ways. Watching your child use the skills you teach them about how to handle being highly sensitive, how to prevent overwhelm, and how to love themselves as an empath can be a magical experience for parents.

Clearly, it can also be challenging to have to teach other people about your child's sensitivities, and to separate your emotions from your child's. Additionally, avoiding exposing your child to your stress, fears, and anxieties is especially important. This can be a challenge for parents, but is an important factor while parenting an empath child.

Empath Mad Libs

Empaths are often serious people. It is important for empath parents and children alike to find the humor in our lives, and it can be especially helpful to laugh about our empath experiences. A fun and easy way to do this with our empath children is to complete an empath Mad Lib together.

Take some time with your child to fill out this empath Mad Lib below. Enjoy some laughter and silliness together, and notice how it changes your energy and the energy of your child.

Once upon a time, there was a _____ empath named _____.
                                    (adjective)   (child's name)

This _____ empath lived in a _____ _____. _____
         (adjective)   (adjective)   (noun)   (child's name)

had amazing superpowers like _____, _____, and _____.
                                (intuitive gift or clair) (intuitive gift or clair)   (intuitive gift or clair)

_____ also had very keen senses.
   (child's name)

They were especially good at _____ and _____.
                                    (1 of 5 senses)   (1 of 5 senses)

_____ liked to use these keen senses to _____ until their
   (child's name)   (verb)

_____ was sore and _____. For _____ to stay happy,
   (body part)   (adjective)   (child's name)

they practiced _____ every morning, and at night they _____.
                     (activity)   (activity)

They were very close to _____, and together, they loved to practice their
                              (parent's name)

superpowers by _____ at the _____.
                  (verb ending in -ing)   (noun)

Passing on Your Empath Wisdom

Many empaths do not discover that they are an empath until they are adults. Only then can they start to fully understand their sensitivities and intuitive abilities. Empath parents have the gifts of knowledge and experience to pass on to their empath children. This information is a priceless gift for the empath child.

1. Think about when you were younger. What are some things about being an empath that you wish you had known back then?

_____

_____

_____

2. What are some ways that you might teach your empath child these things?

_____

_____

_____

3. What are some techniques that you have used to stay grounded and healthy, which you could share with your child?

_____

_____

_____

4. What would you like your child to know about the benefits of being an empath?

_____

_____

_____

5. What are three things that you and your empath child could do together to stay healthy? (Examples: eating healthy, meditating.)

_____

_____

_____

6. What are a few ways in which you could encourage your child's creative side?

_____

_____

_____

7. What would you like your empath child to know about alone time?

_____

_____

_____

8. What can you teach your child about self-care?

_____

_____

_____

KEY LESSONS AND REFLECTION

→ Expressing gratitude has been shown to be an effective way to improve family relationships.

→ One of the most important things empath parents can do for themselves and their children is to learn to separate their own emotions from those of their children.

→ Another important thing empath parents can do is learn to manage their own stress.

→ Tapping and energy healing/energy medicine techniques are great ways to help you and your children deal with stress and challenging emotions.

→ Specific crystals, stones, and gems can be used to help you regulate your energy and emotions and to protect yourself from unhealthy energies.

Reflection Questions

1. What is one thing in this chapter that you are excited to try?

_____

_____

_____

_____

_____

2. In what ways can you incorporate humor into teaching your child about being an empath?

_____

_____

_____

_____

3. How do you feel about using energy healing (energy medicine) techniques for yourself, and teaching them to your child?

_____

_____

_____

_____

_____

4. Which crystals sound most interesting to you and how would you use them in your everyday life?

_____

_____

_____

_____

_____

CHAPTER 5

Empath at Work

In this chapter we focus on some of the challenges that empaths face in regard to work, as well as some of the benefits to being an empath in the workplace. This chapter will help you narrow down potential career paths based on your sensitivities and intuitive gifts. We cover why burnout is especially important for empaths to watch out for, and how to prevent becoming burned out and exhausted. We'll also review some dietary supplements that may assist in reducing the effects of stress, plus several techniques to reduce work-related stress.

LEAD WITH YOUR STRENGTHS

Being an empath gives you several advantages in the workplace. Empaths feel the emotions of others, and we are able to use this information to know when to approach or avoid other people in the workplace. People who are skilled at understanding others' emotions and individual circumstances, like empaths, are more likely to be viewed as effective leaders. In fact, the Management Research Group, which produces management assessment tools and tracks assessment results, found that empathy was the single strongest predictor of ethical leadership.

Empaths are frequently sought out and recognized for teamwork, in part because we are good communicators. Empathetic leaders motivate teams to do their best work. They are great listeners, and they naturally recognize other people's needs and their contributions. Empaths easily cultivate a shared vision among colleagues, as a result of their investment in their team.

Although the impact of technology is growing, our need for human connection is timeless. When an empath represents a company, they naturally show altruism and concern for others, which makes them stand out from the rest.

Clarifying Your Goals

This exercise is designed to get you thinking about how being an empath relates to and impacts your job/career/school.

1.   What are some of the things that you feel good about, in relation to your job/career/school?

_____

_____

_____

2.   In what way(s) do you get meaning out of your job/career/school?

_____

_____

_____

3.   How does being an empath benefit you in your job/career/school?

_____

_____

_____

4.   What are some of the challenges you face in relation to your job/career/school?

_____

_____

_____

5.   What are three to five things you could do to improve upon these challenges?

_____

_____

_____

_____

Supplements for the Empath

Work and school are the top sources of stress for many empaths. When we face stress that is unremitting, we pay with our physical and emotional health. In fact, high levels of stress can cause adrenal fatigue. Adrenal fatigue occurs when the body is in fight-or-flight mode for long periods of time. This causes the body to produce vast amounts of cortisol, preventing the body from making other hormones that we need to manage our stress. Symptoms of adrenal fatigue include insomnia, chronic muscle pain, headaches, depression or anxiety, and exhaustion that is not remedied through sleep.

Although a healthy, balanced diet is paramount, some dietary supplements can be helpful in managing our emotional health, and in combating the effects of adrenal fatigue.

Below, place an X in the box next to the symptoms that bother you. The numbers in parentheses correspond to the supplements list. After identifying some potentially helpful supplements, you can consult a trained holistic health professional, such as a naturopathic physician or a physician who practices integrative medicine, to confirm whether these supplements are right for you. **(Please note that the results of this exercise are intended to be a starting point—not a substitute for guidance from a qualified professional.)**

- ☐ Stomach or bowel issues (1)
- ☐ Low energy (2, 4)
- ☐ Muscle pain (7)
- ☐ Insomnia (7, 10)
- ☐ Sadness or depressed mood (3, 5, 6)
- ☐ Feeling stressed out (4, 7, 10)
- ☐ Trouble concentrating (3, 4, 8)
- ☐ Anxiety (5, 7, 10)
- ☐ Getting sick easily (6, 9, 10)

1. Licorice root

Licorice root has been found to regulate cortisol, improve energy levels, and soothe gastrointestinal problems. It can also speed up the repair of the stomach lining when it is injured due to food poisoning or stomach ulcers.

2. Vitamin D

Low levels of vitamin D have been linked to cortisol overproduction. Vitamin D helps with creating serotonin in the body, thus improving mood.

3. Phosphatidylserine

Phosphatidylserine has been shown to balance cortisol overproduction. Several studies have shown that phosphatidylserine is especially good at regulating and balancing out cortisol levels following exercise.

4. Rhodiola rosea

Rhodiola rosea is an adaptogenic herb known for its capacity to alter hormones and has been found to improve mental performance and energy levels.

5. Ashwagandha

Ashwagandha is also an adaptogenic herb. It has been scientifically found to improve one's resistance toward stress, counteract the physical symptoms of stress, and decrease depression and anxiety.

6. Tyrosine

Tyrosine is an amino acid, and a precursor to feel-good neurotransmitters like dopamine. Tyrosine has been found to help neurotransmitters in the production of dopamine and norepinephrine, and support the body's response to stress.

7. Magnesium

Magnesium deficiency is very common among empaths. Magnesium has been shown to promote relaxation, reduce muscle pain, and improve sleep.

8. Holy basil leaf

Native to Southeast Asia, holy basil leaf acts as an adaptogen. It has been found to improve cognitive function, and improve cortisol levels.

9. Vitamin C

The adrenal glands contain one of the highest concentrations of vitamin C in the body. It has been shown to lower blood pressure, speed up cortisol recovery, and lower stress.

10. L-theanine

L-theanine has been shown to increase feelings of calm, improve sleep and relaxation, and boost the immune system.

AVOIDING BURNOUT

Burnout is a state of exhaustion caused by prolonged stress that negatively impacts your emotional, physical, and mental well-being. Burnout is most often associated with working outside the home, but anyone who feels overworked and undervalued is at risk for feeling burned out. Burnout can happen to the bank teller who has not taken a vacation in two years, or to the stay-at-home mom who balances kids, housework, shopping, and cooking.

Burnout reduces productivity and causes a lack of physical and emotional energy. It can leave you feeling cynical, angry, apathetic, resentful, and dreading the future. You might feel like you have nothing to contribute if burnout goes unaddressed. Burnout can also cause changes to your body that make you more vulnerable to getting sick with cold- or flu-like illnesses.

Empaths are at especially high risk of burnout. Many empaths are drawn to professions like nursing or counseling. Others find themselves in helping roles within office jobs, as they are compassionate and make time to assist others. However, carrying around the emotions of others, as well as the vibes of the physical environment, on top of their own stressors can cause the empath to become burned out quickly.

Are You Burned Out?

Are you experiencing burnout? Place an X in the box if the sentence resonates with you.

- ☐ Every day is a bad day.
- ☐ I am exhausted all the time.
- ☐ The majority of my day is filled with things that are mind-numbing or overwhelming.
- ☐ I feel unappreciated for the work I do.
- ☐ I dread going to work.
- ☐ I get sick more easily than other people.
- ☐ I am tired, but I have trouble falling asleep.
- ☐ I have body aches and pains regularly.
- ☐ I feel unmotivated in regard to my work.
- ☐ I do not feel like I am accomplishing much.
- ☐ I have been isolating myself from others.
- ☐ I have been going to work late or coming home early lately.
- ☐ I use food, drugs, or alcohol to cope with work-related stress.

If you checked off six or more boxes, it is likely that you are burned out.

What Have You Done for You Lately?

What can you do this year to decrease burnout? Take a look at the suggestions below. Circle those that you have already done in the last 12 months.

Take a vacation

Take a mental health day

Take regular breaks at work

Get more hours of sleep

Meditate

Practice deep breathing

Set healthy boundaries at work

Ask for a raise

Allow time for recreation

Learn a new hobby

Immerse yourself in nature

Spend time near a body of water

Eat in a mindful, healthy way

Get a massage

Utilize social supports

Exercise regularly

Reduce exposure to energy vampires

Attend coaching or counseling

Communicate to colleagues what your needs are

Now commit to doing at least four of these suggestions that you have not yet already tried. Write them down here:

_____

_____

_____

_____

_____

_____

_____

DEEPER PRACTICE:
LAUGHTER REALLY IS THE BEST MEDICINE

They say that laughter is the best medicine. As it turns out, laughter is also the stress medicine.

When we laugh, our oxygen intake increases, stimulating the release of endorphins. A good laugh fires up and then cools down your stress response, which will increase then decrease your heart rate and lower your blood pressure. Laughing also stimulates circulation, which helps the muscles relax. According to the Mayo Clinic, laughter can release neuropeptides in your body, which help fight stress and stress-related illnesses. A good belly laugh also provides pain relief, as it causes the body to produce its own natural painkillers: endorphins. Laughing has also been shown to decrease levels of depression and anxiety.

There are great meditation groups designed specifically to get you laughing. If you cannot find a laughing meditation group in your area, you can find laughing meditation videos online. I have listed one of my favorites in the Resources section.

PROTECTING YOUR ENERGY
IN A BUSY WORKPLACE

The time spent by managers and employees in collaborative activities has increased by 50 percent or more over the last two decades, according to the *Harvard Business Review*. The publication also said that "at most companies, 75 percent of employees' days were spent communicating with coworkers, supervisors, or clients."

Empaths, like nonempaths, are spending much of their work hours with others through video conferencing and in-person meetings. For most empaths, even the idea of working closely with others for long periods of time can be tiresome, given how easily they're affected by others' emotions and energies. But working collaboratively does not have to be a nightmare. Here are some steps you can take to keep yourself balanced and centered in any busy work environment.

→ Do the "Eggshell Visualization" (page 26) before going into a meeting—even just a one-on-one meeting, virtual or in-person. Regularly revisualize your protective shell throughout your workday. You can do so whenever you think of it or at specific times, such as when you take breaks or every time you go to the bathroom.

→ Wear jewelry containing crystals or other stones for protection and clearing, or carry a key stone or two in a pocket. (See page 92 and the following exercise for stone recommendations.)

→ If you're sensitive to smells, check your company's employee handbook or with your human resources department for policies on wearing perfume, using highly scented lotions and cosmetics, and using air fresheners in your workplace. If your company doesn't have guidelines about scented products, you can advocate for them.

→ If you're sensitive to sound, download apps or albums with white noise or soothing nature sounds that you can listen to through headphones as you work, in order to help yourself stay calm, as well as tune out distracting noises.

→ Get outside as often as your work allows. Going for a walk or eating lunch outside not only gives you a break from your work setting, but also gives you a quick hit of nature.

→ Keep a plant in your workspace. Studies have shown that plants in the workplace reduce stress while boosting creativity and productivity, among other benefits.

→ If you are currently working from home, chances are you have more control over your work environment. However, sharing workspaces with partners, children, or roommates can also cause sensory and emotional overstimulation. Be sure to take breaks and find alone time to recharge.

Five Ways to Clear Other People's Energy While at Work

Here are a few more techniques for keeping other people's energies and emotions from affecting you at work.

1. **Wash your hands, using cold water, making sure to include your wrists.** As you do this, imagine any emotions or energies from others washing away from you.

2. **Plant your feet on the floor.** Imagine roots growing out the bottom of your feet. The roots go down, deep into the earth below you. Keep this visualization in your mind until you feel like you couldn't be knocked over with a small push from someone. (For more about grounding, see page 132.)

3. **Imagine a ball of white light over your head.** This ball of light is sucking up any energies or emotions that are not yours. You can move this ball of light from your head, slowly down your body, and watch it change color as it cleans your body of other people's energy and emotions. Continue this visualization until you feel cleared of others' energy/emotions.

4. **Carry a black obsidian stone with you to work.** Obsidian is a very good repellent of negative energy or emotions that come from others. When you feel the others' negativity, put the stone in your hands and imagine the stone clearing you, and the space around you. The stone acts like a bug repellent, forcing all negative energies to leave your personal space.

5. **Shake your body.** Find a place that you have just to yourself for two minutes. Even a bathroom stall will do. Clear out other people's energies and/or emotions by shaking your body. As you shake, notice your body releasing other people's energy. Notice how your body becomes more alive and energized.

A Self-Care Toolbox for Work

I enjoy my coaching work with HSPs and empathic people; however, it can be stressful at times. I keep a self-care toolbox in my office, and I dive into it at least once a week. My self-care toolbox is a pretty cardboard storage box that I have filled with little goodies to brighten my day. Currently in my toolbox are a fancy chocolate bar, a bottle of nail polish, a coloring book, a scented candle, a photo of a great vacation, my favorite tea, and some wonderful hand lotion.

Your office self-care toolbox can be a basket, a bag, or a desk drawer. Your toolbox can even be a pocket of your clothing, if you don't have your own individual workspace. The idea is to keep items that appeal to your five senses. The items in your toolbox should be things that you do not normally use. For example, my favorite tea costs a small fortune, so I drink it only when I am mindfully practicing self-care. That way, drinking tea feels like a tiny vacation from the stress of my workday. I find that I am able to brush off any negative energy or stress with ease after using something from my toolbox.

Below are some ideas for things to keep in your toolbox. Circle the ones that appeal to you <u>and that will suit your work environment</u>, and add a few ideas of your own.

Book	Favorite quotes	Love letter
Bubbles	Fidget toys	Markers/pens
Crystals	Fuzzy socks	Sidewalk chalk
Essential oils	Journal	Silly Putty
Face mask	Kite	Snack

Your ideas:

_____

_____

_____

_____

CHOOSING THE RIGHT JOB

Empaths are well regarded in many different careers. However, empathic individuals need to choose a career that supports their temperament and sensitivities, as well as one that utilizes their intuitive gifts. An empath's attributes may be taken for granted in certain settings such as military or government jobs, police work, or in corporate settings. Finding the right position requires considering the company's mission, its goals, who you will be working with, and the physical location and atmosphere. Empaths should use their intuition when deciding on a career. A well-suited position will feel right in your gut.

Empaths generally excel in the helping professions, being self-employed, or working in artistic fields. When empaths take into consideration their sensitivities and intuitive abilities in regard to work, they often feel fulfilled and have a sense of purpose and pride. Empaths are often drawn to become nurses, doctors, chiropractors, counselors, coaches, physical therapists, veterinarians, and dentists because of their desire to help other people. Empaths in these fields tend to do well as long as they give themselves plenty of self-care and make their own emotions and energy a priority.

Additional careers that are good for empaths include graphic design, interior decorating, and advertising. More great options include: independent plumbers or electricians, park/forest rangers, gardeners, working in a gardening center, dog trainers, yoga instructors, massage therapists, and integrative medical providers. Any job that allows empaths to help other people or animals, or allows them to spend time in the outdoors, would likely be a good fit. Having control over your schedule is also a benefit that many empaths seek in their work, because you can make allowances for ample self-care and recreation time.

The Best Job for You

This exercise will help you start identifying careers that you would be well suited for. Write your answers to the following questions.

1. If you could get paid a million dollars a year to do any job you choose, what job would you pick, and why?

    _____

    _____

    _____

2. When you think back to childhood, what did you want to be when you "grew up"? Does this have any meaning to you now?

    _____

    _____

    _____

3. Have others told you that you would be good at a particular career? Which one? Do you agree or disagree?

    _____

    _____

    _____

Career Personality Assessment

This exercise will ask about your personality traits and personal preferences. Based on your answers, I will suggest some jobs/careers that might be a good fit for you.

Read each statement. If you agree with the statement, fill in the circle. There are no wrong answers!

Being around people gives me energy.	○			
I think and reflect before I act.	○			
I have a vivid imagination.			○	
I quickly get involved in the social life of a new workplace.	○			
I trust reason rather than my feelings.				○
I am rarely late to my appointments.	○			
I like to work around targets and deadlines.	○			
I pride myself on ingenuity.				○
I make decisions quickly.			○	
Freedom in my job is important to me.			○	
I like to try new things.			○	
I am fiercely independent.				○
I like to take risks.			○	
I avoid conflict and/or confrontation.		○		
I respect authority, even if I disagree.	○			
I like solving problems.				○
Integrity is very important to me.		○		
I am quite skeptical.				○
I believe in working together for the good of all.		○		

G	S	A	W

Add up the number of filled-in circles in each column and write them in the corresponding box. Note which letter corresponds to your highest score. The letters stand for the following: Guard, Sentinel, Artist, and Watcher.

The Guard: Guards are very serious about their job responsibilities. Guards take pride in being dependable and trustworthy. They are reliable, and they respect authority, even when it might not be in their best interest. Guards are practical and down-to-earth, and they adhere to the rules set out before them. They are good at cooperating with others, and have a sharp eye for following procedures. Guards tend not to blaze new trails, and are cautious about change. Guards do well in engineering, management, work with computers and programming, construction, machinery, and as mechanics.

The Sentinel: Sentinels are great at cooperating and group work. They do their best to avoid conflict and/or confrontation. Sentinels have a unique talent for helping people get along with one another and work together for the good of all. Sentinels value ethics, and they hold themselves to a strict standard of personal integrity. Sentinels tend to thrive with careers in health care, human resources, and human services. Sentinels generally excel in management positions.

The Artist: Artists love working in any of the arts. They have keen senses and they use them to get where they want to go quickly and efficiently. They are bold, and make decisions quickly. They do not need much direction, as they like to fill in the blanks as they go. Artists have a way with people, and seek adventure and novelty. Artists are excellent problem solvers, but they may have trouble doing things that are not fun to them. Artists desire freedom in a work setting, and resist being confined. Artists flourish in fine arts and performing arts. They often enjoy self-employment, but also tend to enjoy work in radio and television, psychology, photography, interior design, and architecture.

The Watcher: Whether solving problems in organic systems such as plants and animals, or in mechanical systems such as railroads and computers, watchers use their analytical skills to solve problems. Watchers are scrupulously logical. They are fiercely independent in their thinking, and tend to be skeptical. Watchers pride themselves on their ingenuity. Watchers do best in careers oriented to business, technology, advertising, marketing, and medicine.

KEY LESSONS AND REFLECTION

→ Empathy is the single strongest predictor of ethical leadership.
→ Adrenal fatigue is caused by prolonged stress and symptoms include bowel issues, insomnia, exhaustion, trouble concentrating, and anxiety or depression.
→ Supplements such as phosphatidylserine, vitamins D and C, and licorice root can aid in adrenal fatigue or chronic stress.
→ At most companies, 75 percent of employees' days are spent communicating with others.
→ Empaths generally excel in the helping professions, being self-employed, or working in artistic fields.

Reflection Questions

1. Are you currently working in a field that is well suited to you, as an empath? If not, are there careers that interest you and may be better suited to your sensitivities and intuitive gifts? What are these?

_____

_____

2. What are some things that you can do to prevent burnout?

_____

_____

3. What are three steps you can complete now toward taking a vacation this year? (For example, request time off from work, or save $10 a week.)

_____

_____

_____

CHAPTER 6

Empath Self-Care

In this chapter we'll cover what self-care is, and why it is important for empathic people. Next, we discuss resiliency, where it comes from, and how to become a more resilient empath.

Part of self-care is learning to love yourself, so I have written a couple of activities for you to deepen your self-love. Breathing techniques that foster self-care are described, as well as grounding techniques and activities. Additionally, we'll address how making connections with others can be a form of self-care.

THE IMPORTANCE OF SELF-CARE

Self-care is the first step toward becoming an empowered empath. An empowered empath can adjust the dial on their senses, turning them up or down as needed. They are able to significantly reduce how much negative emotion they pick up from others. Much of the time, they feel grounded and balanced rather than overwhelmed.

Self-care comes in countless forms. I love getting a massage, but my friend Susan thinks they are painful. Often, you will have to experiment with different forms of self-care to discover what is most effective for you. Anything that "fills up your gas tank" can be considered self-care. From bubble baths to working on cars, if it replenishes your energy or alleviates your stress, it can be called self-care.

Many of my empath clients put everyone else's needs ahead of their own, which leaves little to no time for self-care. This always results in clients feeling overwhelmed and drained. One of my clients, Penny, took care of patients as a nurse while working the night shift at the hospital. After her long and arduous shift, she returned home to care for her 9-year-old autistic daughter. Penny slept very little, and rarely asked for help. Three years went by as she cared for everyone but herself. One day she arrived home from work, picked up her mail, and found that her aunt had sent her some old photographs of Penny and her mother, who had passed away when Penny was a teenager. Penny found herself uncontrollably crying, and she was engulfed in sadness. She poured herself a drink, and then another, and before long she had passed out on the living room floor, which was very uncharacteristic of her. Hours later, she awoke to a loud knock at her door. Still intoxicated, she opened the door to find her daughter, accompanied by two police officers. Penny's daughter had been found wandering barefoot around the neighborhood. Although she was not hurt, Penny had to face several visits with child protection workers, and she had to go to court where she faced child neglect and endangerment charges. She knew that if charged, she might lose her job as well.

Penny came to me absolutely disgusted with herself. Had she asked her family or friends for help or had some form of self-care over the years, she might not have found herself in this terrible situation. As Penny found a self-care routine that worked for her, and prioritized things in her life differently, she grew more joyful, calm, and self-aware. Her relationship with her daughter flourished, and she met a man, fell in love, and got married. Having a self-care routine allowed Penny to restore her vitality. As she took care of herself, she felt more stable, happier, and less anxious. She reported also having more energy to give to the people she loved.

Empath Self-Assessment

To be the best version of themselves, I have found that empaths need:

→ Alone time that is quiet and peaceful
→ Healthy food and/or helpful supplements
→ Meditation, prayer, or mindfulness practices
→ Four relaxing vacations a year (see "Deeper Practice: The Importance of Vacations" on page 122)

1. How many of these things have you done this week?

2. How many of these have you done in the last three months? Six months?

3. What is your main source of self-care? How often do you practice this?

4. When we have only one form of self-care, that form tends to become unhealthy. For example, if I take a nap every time I am stressed, I would be in bed about 20 hours a day! List all the forms of self-care that you currently practice.

DEEPER PRACTICE:
THE IMPORTANCE OF VACATIONS

Elaine Aron, author of *The Highly Sensitive Person*, recommends that HSPs take four vacations a year. This is something I recommend for empaths as well. Most of us cannot afford to take four vacations a year, but there are ways to escape from the hustle and bustle of our lives that don't break the bank. Taking a camping trip is a great and inexpensive way to relax. A road trip to visit a friend who will give you free accommodations would also be an affordable way to take a time-out.

Dr. Aron makes an important point in recommending these vacations be mellow and slow paced. The reason for this is that HSPs, as well as empaths, get overstimulated when they rush from attraction to attraction. Additionally, places that stimulate the senses, like a Vegas casino, can drain the HSP/empath to the degree that they need a vacation after their vacation. New York City is great, but for the HSP and/or empath, a vacation on a beach is a better choice. Having a slow-paced vacation allows the HSP/empath the chance to quiet their mind, relax their bodies, and restore themselves to harmony and balance.

What are three things you can do now, to get one step closer to taking a vacation?

_____

_____

_____

Self-Care Ideas for Empaths

Below are some ideas on what you might do for your self-care. Circle the ones that interest you the most, making sure to choose at least five different activities.

Art	Going to a museum	Playing records
Bath	Happy memories	Playing with a pet
Bike riding	Hiking	Refinishing furniture
Buying/selling stock	Horseback riding	Sewing
Camping	Hunting	Sightseeing
Cooking	Journaling	Singing
Dancing	Knitting	Skydiving
Daydreaming	Learning something	Swimming
Debating	Lighting candles	Talking to spirit guides
Deep breathing	Listening to music	Time with a friend
Doing puzzles	Massage	Traveling
Doing your makeup	Meditation	Walking
Eating a nice meal	Movie	Working on a vehicle
Fishing	Napping	Writing
Fixing something	Photography	Writing a letter
Gardening	Picnicking	Yoga
Giving a gift	Planning a trip	
Going for a drive	Playing an instrument	

Next, on the calendar on page 124, number the days according to the current month. Then, place self-care activities onto the calendar, committing to two to three per week.

MONTHLY CALENDAR EXAMPLE

SUN	MON	TUES	WED	THU	FRI	SAT
				Journal		*Hike*
Yoga		*Work on art*				
	Work on art		*Journal*			*Yoga*
Epsom salt bath		*Catch up with friends*				*Work on art*
Journal			*Lunch with friend*	*Yoga*		

SUN	MON	TUES	WED	THU	FRI	SAT

DEEPER PRACTICE: AROMATHERAPY

Aromatherapy is a great way to help an empath feel their best. Many oils are used to help reduce stress, nausea, discomfort, or pain, and to help us fall and stay asleep. Four aromatherapy oils have been determined to be both safe and effective for use by anyone over age five: ginger, lavender, orange, and peppermint.

Ginger essential oil is said to eliminate toxins, ease stomach discomfort, and enhance appetite. It is commonly used to help clear the respiratory tract. Ginger is also known for soothing aches and pains in the muscles, and reducing inflammation.

Lavender is known to be effective in calming anxiety. Lavender essential oil promotes relaxation and improves sleep. It is also believed that lavender essential oil can be used to treat anxiety, fungal infections, allergies, depression, and eczema.

Orange essential oil has a mood-lifting effect and has been shown to improve blood flow. Because it improves circulation, it may be helpful in managing headaches as well.

Peppermint essential oil has been found to eliminate harmful bacteria, relieve muscle spasms and flatulence, and aid in reducing muscle tension when used in a massage. When peppermint essential oil is mixed with a carrier oil (an oil used to dilute other oils) and rubbed into the feet, it can work as a natural fever reducer.

Experiment with different types of essential oils to see what you like best. Aromatherapy works only if you enjoy the oil's smell and find it to be helpful. People have different smell preferences and associations.

Essential oils can be put into a diffuser, a device that disperses the oil into the air as a fine mist, so that you can inhale them safely. When essential oils are diffused into the air, the oils' compounds are absorbed through olfactory receptors in the nose. Messages are sent to the brain through the olfactory system and are said to affect the limbic system, which plays a role in our emotions.

Cautions

→ Never allow young children access to essential oils without supervision.

→ If you're highly sensitive to smell, you may become overwhelmed with strong-smelling oils. In this case, do not use aromatherapy; stick to essential oils that do not trigger negative effects.

→ Essential oils are highly concentrated and can be toxic if swallowed.

→ Many essential oils can also be harmful if they are applied in pure form (undiluted) to the skin.

→ If you have health conditions, please consult with a health professional before trying aromatherapy.

BUILD YOUR INNER RESILIENCY

All of us face challenges in life, ranging in severity from a flat tire, to something as life changing as sexual assault. What seems like a small setback to one person may seem like a monumental punch in the gut to someone else. Nevertheless, even the most agonizing situation won't keep us down forever. We tend to bounce back given time and a little resilience.

Resilience is the process of adapting, even flourishing, in the face of adversity, tragedy, death, divorce, or other stress. I believe that our exponential growth, or flourishing, comes from the personal growth that occurs frequently during our most painful moments. I have always said that breakups look good on me, because when dumped, I am forced to take a long hard look at myself. After I stop crying, I have to make changes that allow me to be a better partner in the next relationship.

Although these painful events are a guaranteed part of life, they do not have to determine your mood, your physical health, or your outlook. Becoming more resilient allows you to more easily navigate difficult times. Resilience is necessary for the kind of emotional growth that tends to occur as we face life's trials.

Examining Your Resiliency

This exercise will help you understand when you have exhibited resiliency in the past, and some of your fears around future resiliency.

1. Many empaths experience abuse from a narcissistic parent. If you experienced this, what created the resilience in you that allowed you to survive?

_____

_____

_____

2. What other situations have required that you be resilient?

_____

_____

_____

3. Are there any situations that you fear you could not survive?

_____

_____

_____

4. What is it about this situation that scares you?

_____

_____

_____

5. What are three ways that you could build your resilience in regard to the feared situation(s)?

_____

_____

_____

CULTIVATING RESILIENCE

Resilience does not involve any specific set of behaviors or actions; thus, it varies from person to person. A great way to determine how you can develop resilience is to look at a resilient person you know and ask them what they have done to develop their resilience. If no one comes to mind, look at the common characteristics resilient people share that seem to have developed their resilience, and try to emulate them. Additionally, it is important to build upon your strengths. It can be any strength that you see in yourself: from "You are a great lie detector" to "You have beautiful hair."

Although building on your resilience looks different for everyone, I will share some more specific practices that I have witnessed while building a client's resilience. Developing a sense of purpose for your life is one of the practices to building or strengthening resilience that seems to be effective for empathic people. Developing a stronger sense of community has also been helpful to my clients when developing resilience, as they feel more connected to, and valued in, their community. Last but not least, keep things in perspective! Rather than making generalizations like "I am never going to be happy," say instead, "I have been depressed for a month, but I have come out of it before, and I can do it again."

Develop Self-Love

The most effective way to build resilience, in my opinion, is to work on loving yourself. Too many empaths are kind to everyone but themselves. Often, I have to ask my clients this question: If your best friend came to you with the same circumstances you are describing in your life, what would your advice to them be? Clients always respond similarly, by saying that they would be compassionate, understanding, and validating. I cannot find any evidence that shows that self-hate is helpful in any way. There are, however, mounds of evidence that illustrate that positive self-talk improves mood, relationships, motivation, sleep, and self-esteem and decreases anxiety and depression.

Developing Love for Yourself

This activity will help you examine your resiliency and how you might build upon this to become even more resilient.

First, identify a core belief you have about yourself that is negative. A core belief is a belief about yourself that usually stems from childhood. It is inflexible and strongly held, and is maintained by the tendency to focus only on information and experiences that support it, while ignoring the things that do not.

For example, my coaching client Kahlil had a core belief that he was unlikable. Anytime he perceived a slight from a friend, he reinforced this core belief by telling himself that because he is unlikable, his friends did not invite him to the movie, or whatever the "slight" was. Kahlil ignored the 53 other times that he was invited to join his friends, and focused only on events that supported his core belief. Your core belief, then, could be something related to your personality, behavior, history, relationships, or any other part of you. Common core beliefs among empaths are that they are crazy, unlovable, too much to handle, or that they are worthless.

Next, use the space below to write a letter to yourself. Write it as though you were talking to your best friend. Be sure to be compassionate and understanding and provide some validation in the letter. Do your best to avoid any generalizations like "I am never going to be happy." Instead, narrow down that sentiment to something smaller, and more specific, like: "I have been in a depressed state for a month."

As you write, follow these guidelines:

1. Although you are writing this letter to yourself about your core belief, do so as though you were writing to the person you love most in the world. This will allow you to find the kindest words for yourself.

2. Think of your biggest "cheerleader." Someone who loves and accepts you unconditionally. What would they say to you about this core belief?

3. Is there any evidence that refutes this core belief? For example: My belief is that I am annoying. Evidence to refute this could be that I have 10 friends. If I have that many friends, how could I possibly be that annoying?

4. Remind yourself where this core belief comes from. If it stems from the past, is it even relevant now?

5. Remind yourself that every single person on the planet has flaws, and there are things about themselves that they don't like. How many people do you think struggle with that same core belief?

6. Consider your genetics. If your dad and grandmother both had bipolar disorder, maybe you should be taking that into account. Also consider your childhood, and any traumas that have occurred over the years that impacted your core belief.

7. After writing your love letter, read it to yourself out loud. How does it feel to hear loving and compassionate words from yourself? You may want to keep the letter somewhere safe and reread it when the core belief resurfaces in the future.

The Self-Validation Vacation

Beating yourself up? Feeling burned out or overwhelmed? The self-validation vacation is here to help. I find in my work that empaths are often excellent at validating the emotions and experiences of others, but often have difficulty validating their own emotions and experiences. When I teach this self-validation exercise, they are amazed at the benefits.

The idea is to identify what you are feeling—such as overwhelmed, anxious, sad, or lonely—and then to validate your experience.

Fill in the blank in this sentence, using your current emotional state:

"Of course I feel _____."

Now list all of the possible reasons that contribute to feeling that way. What you write might look something like this:

Of course I feel depressed because I have been quarantined in my home for four weeks, and have not been able to work. I have had almost zero social interaction during this time, which I thought I would like, but realize I do not. I had an argument with my best friend, and my neighbors keep blaring their music, which really bothers me. I haven't had a good meal in two weeks because I have been scared to go to the grocery store, and I hate cooking for just myself. My dog keeps whining because she wants me to play with her. I think we are both stir-crazy.

The more you practice this exercise, the less you will have to fight negative emotions. I also find that self-validating gives us the permission needed to do further self-care. As you validate your feelings, taking a day to yourself seems like a healthy and reasonable decision, rather than something that is self-indulgent.

Try it yourself:

Of course I feel _____ because _____

_____

_____

_____

_____

_____

_____

Stay Grounded

The earth has an electromagnetic field that causes a compass needle to orient north. This field allows birds to navigate south when colder weather hits. Electromagnetic fields can also be man-made. X-ray machines, TVs, cell phones, and computers all have electromagnetic fields. Similarly, humans have electromagnetic fields.

Grounding practitioners believe that when we connect with the electromagnetic field of the earth, we can reduce pain and fatigue, decrease inflammation, sleep better, and lower the stress hormone cortisol.

This idea should make sense to the most critical skeptics, as the opposite is also scientifically proven. In fact, the World Health Organization classified radio electromagnetic fields as potentially carcinogenic in 2011. Electromagnetic fields can be dangerous not only because of the risk of cancer, but also other health problems, including electromagnetic hypersensitivity (EHS), which is characterized by acute and chronic inflammatory processes in the skin, nervous system, and organ systems, as well as in the respiratory, cardiovascular, and musculoskeletal systems.

Staying grounded is one key element to pulling away from negative emotions. Grounding will allow you to refocus and create space from strong feelings or emotions. It also reduces inflammation and stress, elevates mood, and improves blood flow.

Grounding does not have to be a meditative, bare-feet-on-the-earth-type experience. Going on a nature walk or doing tent camping can also provide a very beneficial grounding experience. Research has shown that taking group nature walks, for example, is linked with lower depression, less stress, and a more positive mood. Other research has shown that spending long stretches of time in the woods—a "forest bath"—can boost the number of white blood cells that fight viruses and tumors.

If you have ever gone camping, and slept close to the earth, you might have noticed the effects of grounding. Improved sleep, lowered stress, reduced anxiety, and/or more energy are common experiences. My friend used to say that no matter how much alcohol he drank, if he slept outside, he would never wake up hungover. I do not recommend putting that claim to the test, but it is a funny anecdote.

Get Grounded

One easy way to ground yourself is to put your bare feet on the earth. Make sure you're actually touching the ground—not pavement. Stand or sit for as long as you're able or that feels good to you.

If going barefoot outside isn't an option, the following grounding practice can be done indoors.

→ Sit down in a comfortable place, making sure that your feet can touch the floor. Close your eyes and focus on your breath. Breathe in slowly for the count of four, then out slowly to the count of five.

→ Next, focus on what you can feel with your body. How do the backs of your legs feel as they touch the place you sit? How about your back? What do your hands feel? Is your head resting on anything? Is the material on the chair/couch/bed smooth or textured? Touch it with your hands, noticing the subtleties.

→ Now draw your attention to your feet. Push your feet into the floor gently. Imagine any negative energy or emotions in your body draining down your body, down your legs, and out your feet, into the floor. Does this emotion or energy have a color? Texture?

→ As it moves down your body, notice how heavy each body part becomes, how relaxed. Imagine all of that energy and emotion leaving your body, draining out your feet and into the floor.

→ Enjoy the relaxation in your body. Take three more deep breaths in and three breaths out. When you are ready, you can open your eyes and return to the room.

After completing this exercise, take some time to answer the following questions:

1. Were you able to imagine what the energy or emotion looked like? If so, describe it here:

_____

_____

_____

2. How were you feeling prior to this grounding exercise? What about after?

_____

_____

_____

3. What, if anything, would you add or change about this grounding technique that would enhance its effects for you?

_____

_____

Know Your Media and Technology Triggers

Empaths can feel the energies and emotions of others through various forms of technology—watching television, hearing a podcast, and sometimes even through reading an email. It is important for empaths to be mindful of the tone and energy of the media that they are exposed to, and to limit the exposure to things that induce negative emotions.

Empaths differ on what they perceive as a trigger to negative emotions. For example, watching a hunting program may be a pleasant way to entertain one empath, whereas another empath may experience sadness or anxiety while watching. The most common technology and media triggers that my clients report include horror movies, political debates, true crime, boxing or other aggressive sports, heavy metal music, advertising, and social media.

The evening news tends to focus on the latest tragedy or disaster, thus many empaths experience negative emotions when they watch it. I had a client who valued staying updated on current events, but who had terrible anxiety while watching the news. She came up with a perfect solution: She skipped the news, and instead watched a late-night talk show, where all the major current events were covered, but in a humorous way. She was able to stay informed, and reduced her anxiety significantly simply by getting the news from a different source.

There is plenty of research that correlates low self-esteem, poor body image, depression, and anxiety to checking your social media. An Austrian study found that just scrolling through Facebook for 20 minutes prompts a depressant effect on mood. Many studies suggest that the more time someone spends on social media, the higher their rates of depression and anxiety. In fact, using Facebook even correlates with reduced satisfaction in all areas of life. It is important to say that correlation is not the same as causation. It could be that depressed or anxious people may just spend more time on social media platforms. It is critical for the empath, then, to be mindful of their emotions before, during, and after they spend time on social media.

Consider reducing or eliminating your exposure, for one week, to anything that elicits a negative mood. I did this years ago, and haven't watched the news since. Keep in mind that our environments affect us in profound ways. Be mindful of your emotional responses to your environment. Minimizing your exposure to things that evoke negative feelings will make a massive difference in your emotional state.

Technology Tracker

In the table below, record all the media you are exposed to for one day. Write down your activity during each hour of the day, your corresponding mood, and any thoughts or observations you want to remember. When you identify something that inspires in you a negative mood, set a goal to reduce, limit, or eliminate that trigger, and write your goal in the box next to it.

EXAMPLE

TIME	ACTIVITY	MOOD	THOUGHTS	GOALS
7–8 a.m.	Listened to music, prepared for work	Good, normal mood	The music I chose was upbeat and happy	None
8–9 a.m.	Arrived at work, read magazine article about spaying/neutering pets	Sad, a little hopeless	Article discussed the number of pets that need homes—not a "happy"-inducing activity	Avoid my exposure to sad animal stories, articles, and commercials. Do not listen to Sarah McLachlan

TIME	ACTIVITY	MOOD	THOUGHTS	GOALS
7–8 a.m.				
8–9 a.m.				
9–10 a.m.				
10–11 a.m.				
11 a.m.–12 p.m.				
12–1 p.m.				
1–2 p.m.				
2–3 p.m.				
3–4 p.m.				
4–5 p.m.				
5–6 p.m.				
6–7 p.m.				
7–8 p.m.				
8–9 p.m.				
9–10 p.m.				
10–11 p.m.				

Connection with Other Empaths

It is important for empaths to connect in some way to other empathic people. Meeting another empath who lives near you, and who can interact in a face-to-face setting, is ideal, but there are many other options such as online groups and social media groups that are dedicated to supporting empaths.

Connections of this sort are helpful for many reasons. First, empathic people will understand you and how you experience the world in a way that nonempaths cannot. This helps you feel validated and, in my experience, helps you shift the focus from feeling drained to enjoying the fun parts of being an empath. Another empath can make suggestions about the unique hurdles you both face, and it is fun to practice our intuitive gifts with people who share them.

Ultimately, having one empath friend or an entire empath community helps us to thrive.

Making New Connections

It can be challenging to find other empaths. Heck, it can be hard to make new friends, empath or not! The more people we meet, or get to know, the greater our chances of meeting other empaths.

Below is a list of suggestions to help you make new connections. Take a look, and circle any of the activities you have done in the last five years.

Join the Facebook group "Dr. Orloff's Empath Support Community" (maintained by Judith Orloff, MD, author of *The Empath's Survival Guide*)

Look at local gatherings on the website Meetup (meetup.com)

Take a class at a hardware store

Take a class at a craft store

Volunteer

Take a vacation with a group

Attend or start a local empath group

Take your dog to the dog park

Play a group sport

Join a book club

Take a group class at the gym

Attend a religious or spiritual group

Take a class at your local community college

Go dancing

See live music

Go to a lake or swimming pool

Host a dinner or game night

Invite neighbors over

Now answer the following questions:

1. How many activities from the list did you circle?

---

2. If you circled fewer than four, maybe it is time to put yourself out there. Are any of the suggested activities appealing to you? If so, which ones?

---

3. What is one thing that you can do right now that would put you a step closer to doing one of these activities?

DEEPER PRACTICE:
ORGONITE FOR THE EMPATH

Orgonite has become very popular as a spiritual healing tool and as protection against electromagnetic pollution. Orgonite is simply a 50/50 mix of resin and metal. Often, it contains quartz or other crystals as well. Orgonite is said to draw in negative energy and transmute it into positive energy. The resin in orgonite shrinks during the curing process, permanently squeezing the quartz crystal inside. As a result, its endpoints become polarized inside the crystal—known as the piezoelectric effect—causing it to function more effectively as a positive energy generator.

Various healing practices incorporate the idea of manipulating the subtle energies in and around us for better health. Such energy might be called orgone, or qi, in traditional Chinese medicine. Ayurveda practitioners call this energy prana. Whatever we name it, the effects are the same, and can be beneficial to empaths.

User-Reported Benefits of Orgonite

- → Improves sleep
- → Reduces stress
- → Increases spiritual growth
- → Creates a more harmonious home or work environment
- → Protects people from negative energies such as electromagnetic frequencies
- → Clears emotional and/or energetic blocks
- → Increases resiliency to illness
- → Balances sensitivity in empathic individuals

You can make orgonite yourself fairly easily, as most of the ingredients are found in nature. If that sounds too time consuming, you can purchase it online from various places including Amazon, Etsy, and private sellers. I have provided additional information in the Resources section, including links to instructions for how to make orgonite yourself.

Qigong, Tai Chi, and Yoga for Empaths

Physical activity stimulates the production of dopamine, norepinephrine, and serotonin in your brain. These are the chemicals that generate positive emotions. Certain physical activities seem deigned to use up energy associated with stress, anxiety, and other negative emotions. Qigong (pronounced Chee-GUNG), tai chi, and yoga are three of these activities.

Qigong is a self-healing energy practice derived from traditional Chinese medicine that aims to balance life energy, or chi. Chinese medicine asserts that energy blockages are the cause of mental and physical illness, and qigong will clear such blockages.

Tai chi is often described as "meditation in motion." There is growing evidence that this mind-body practice can be used to treat many health problems. You can practice tai chi even if you aren't in great shape, as it is very gentle and low impact. While practicing tai chi, your muscles are relaxed rather than tensed, and your joints are never fully extended, making this an exercise that anyone can do.

Yoga, like qigong, has many variants. The rewards of yoga practices are many: physical, emotional, spiritual, and social, when practiced with others. Because empaths tend to have a rather dissociative relationship with their bodies, practicing yoga is especially good for us. The mindful yogic sequences require attention to and focus on your body, and the accompanying breathing techniques will slow your heart rate and bring your nervous system to baseline.

In the Resources section, I've included links to one online video for each of these three activities. Go ahead and try each for yourself. Make note of how you feel doing the activity and after. Make a commitment to do one of the three activities on a regular basis.

KEY LESSONS AND REFLECTION

→ Anything that "fills up your gas tank" can be considered self-care.
→ Resilience is the process of adapting, even flourishing, in the face of adversity, tragedy, death, divorce, or other stress.
→ Grounding will allow you to refocus and create space from strong feelings or emotions.
→ Self-validation makes doing self-care easier.
→ Qigong, tai chi, and yoga are physical activities that use up energy associated with negative emotions.

Reflection Questions

1. How many close connections do you have? Would you enjoy having either more social connections, or connections with other empaths?

_____

_____

_____

2. If you answered yes in question 1, what are two ways that you will try to expand your social circle?

_____

_____

_____

3. If you were to unplug from social media, the news, and other sources of negativity, how would you spend your extra time?

_____

_____

_____

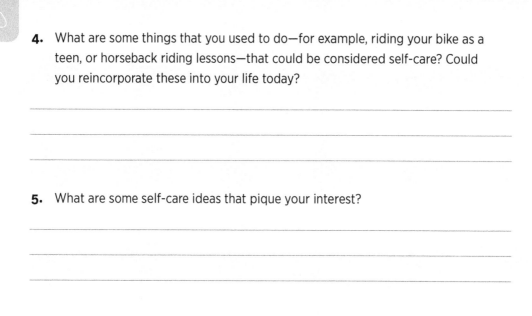

4. What are some things that you used to do—for example, riding your bike as a teen, or horseback riding lessons—that could be considered self-care? Could you reincorporate these into your life today?

_____

_____

_____

5. What are some self-care ideas that pique your interest?

_____

_____

_____

Empath Thriving

In this chapter we reflect back on what we have learned so far. We take a broader perspective on what makes someone an empath and examine a possible purpose for your time here on Earth. We talk about a more spiritual perspective on the empath and the effect that they have on others, the environment, and the energy around them. We also discuss how your emotions create your energetic frequency, and how this frequency draws to you people and objects that have the same vibration.

TODAY AND BEYOND

Applying the strategies that you have learned in this workbook daily will allow you to live a happy, joyful, and fulfilling life. Utilizing what you have learned, come up with a daily routine that includes self-care, preventive strategies, and techniques that ground and center you after a draining situation. Incorporating these tools will help you face day-to-day life with some gas in your tank and some pep in your step. As you experience living life as an empowered empath, notice how your intuitive gifts become stronger. When we regularly practice the techniques that make us feel grounded, we shift from surviving to thriving.

Reflections

Take some time now to look back at the strategies you tried in this book. As you examine them, make note of the ones that were most helpful. Below are some questions that will get you thinking about how to incorporate these into your daily life.

1. Which activities in this workbook stand out to you as most helpful?

2. What would you say is the most important thing you learned so far from the workbook?

3. Which of the techniques in the workbook are you willing to apply to your life on a weekly basis? Daily? Monthly? Yearly?

4. What are three things you could do to ensure that you use your favorite skills as frequently as you intend?

_____

_____

_____

5. What is one technique in the workbook that you can commit to learning more about?

_____

6. Is there anyone you would like to choose to hold you accountable for practicing your favorite techniques from the workbook? If so, who? How might they go about this?

_____

_____

7. What is one way to reward yourself for regularly incorporating the skills?

_____

DID YOU VOLUNTEER TO COME HERE?

Dolores Cannon, a hypnotherapist who specialized in past life regression, discovered through her work that the earth and its people were in need of help. Souls were given the opportunity to volunteer and come to Earth to help bring the world into a new state of consciousness.

There are three waves of volunteers. The first wave includes people from the 1940s through the 1970s who are called indigos. The "crystal children" who form the second wave were born during the 1970s and 1980s. The third wave is a group of exceptional new children, many of whom are currently in their teens. These volunteers are called "rainbow children," and most were born between 1990 and 2020.

There are outliers: People born outside of these time frames may also fall into these three waves of volunteers.

What does this have to do with the empath? *I believe* all empaths—even those not born in Cannon's three waves—are highly evolved souls who heard the call sent out for volunteers. We raised our hands and agreed to help humanity and the planet. We knew that humanity and the planet could not be helped without us. We came here, to a place that is full of pain and despair, anger and abuse, manipulation and materialism, and often, because it's so different from the place we came from, we struggle with depression and anxiety here. When I discovered that I was an indigo child, I suddenly understood why I have battled depression throughout my life.

All empaths have the power to help the earth, animals, and other humans to heal, and they do so in many different ways. Many empaths act as a mirror to others in order for them to work on the attributes of their personality that need healing. Some empaths make their way into careers that allow them to heal others. No matter how you are helping, know that you are part of a collective team, and you are not alone. Whether you are helping the world consciously or not, it makes no difference. It is your energy, not your behavior, that is healing the world.

DEEPER PRACTICE:
UNDERSTANDING THE THREE WAVES
OF VOLUNTEERS

Some empaths came to Earth with one of the three waves of volunteers, and some did not. The three waves of volunteers are no better or worse than an empath who came here outside of the three waves. What distinguishes empaths who did arrive here in one of the three waves is simply that their mission here is directed toward a more specific purpose.

For example, indigo children have a strong tendency toward tearing down old systems that either no longer work well in today's society or that no longer make sense. As an indigo child myself, I struggled with the "rules" that were placed on me as a licensed professional counselor. I let my license expire and became a coach instead so I could do things like hug my clients, recommend vitamins/supplements, and discuss alternatives to Western medicine. My indigo side came on full force when dealing with the licensing board and its rules that I considered an impediment to my clients' health. I have done some work on "tearing down" that system, and it continues to play out today. Like many indigo children, I feel called to abolish systems that are not serving the greater good.

Many indigos have trouble adjusting to life here and find it to be painful. Some even attempt suicide despite their lives appearing fine to others. Of the three waves, the first had the hardest time with the transition from where they came (which was devoid of the pain that exists here) to life here, on Earth.

The second wave, or crystal children, came here with a unique energy that heals others. Crystal children walk through busy places while operating as large antennae. They heal everyone around them, whether they are trying to or not. Interestingly, many of the crystal children do not like being around other people, as it can be uncomfortable for them. They unconsciously want to get their job as a volunteer here done and return to the place from which they came. For that reason, many crystal children do not want to marry or have children.

The third wave of volunteers, the rainbow children, are said to have advanced DNA, and they come here with all the knowledge they need. They run on a higher energetic frequency than the rest of us. Many are graduating from college in their teens, starting business ventures, or inventing things. Rainbow children get bored easily in school and need to be challenged intellectually. Sadly, many of them are misdiagnosed as having ADD, ADHD, or being on the autism spectrum. They often get medicated, which is a disservice to them. They are here to assist in the transformation of human DNA that will allow for a higher form of consciousness.

Are You an Indigo, Crystal, or Rainbow Child?

Circle yes or no for each question.

1.	Have you always felt like you were here for a reason?	Yes	No
2.	Do you rely on your intuition when making decisions?	Yes	No
3.	Do you ever have problems/issues with authority?	Yes	No
4.	Do you generally dislike systems? (A "system" is defined as a set of rules to work toward a common goal.)	Yes	No
5.	Do you prefer to be alone, or even isolate?	Yes	No
6.	Have you had two or more addictions (drugs, alcohol, food, shopping, sex, for example)?	Yes	No
7.	Do you have a strong sense of purpose and/or life direction?	Yes	No
8.	Were you born between 1940 and 1979?	Yes	No
9.	Have you been told that you lack patience?	Yes	No
10.	Do you consider yourself to be strong-willed?	Yes	No
11.	Do you suffer from allergies and/or sensitivities caused by environmental factors?	Yes	No
12.	Are you spontaneous to the point of acting without thinking through the consequences first?	Yes	No
13.	Were you born between the 1970s and 1980s?	Yes	No
14.	Are you especially imaginative and/or creative?	Yes	No
15.	Do you feel connected to all of humankind?	Yes	No
16.	Do you still keep in contact with your childhood friends?	Yes	No
17.	Do you love music, but dislike loud noise?	Yes	No
18.	Do you prefer to teach yourself what you want to learn, rather than what you are told to study?	Yes	No
19.	Do you prefer comfort over fashion?	Yes	No

20. Would you say that of the clairs, you are especially
    good at clairvoyance and clairsentience?   Yes   No
21. Do you have a propensity to trip electricity?   Yes   No
22. Are you gay, bisexual, or gender fluid?   Yes   No
23. Would you say that you don't care much
    what people think of you?   Yes   No
24. Are you able to detect danger before it happens?   Yes   No
25. Do you believe in the ability to levitate,
    to teleport, or in telepathy?   Yes   No
26. Were you born after the year 1990?   Yes   No
27. Are you good with technology and do you easily
    figure out new gadgets?   Yes   No
28. Have others told you that you seem to be in your own world? Yes   No
29. Are you brave, or particularly able to withstand hardship? Yes   No
30. Were you late to start speaking?   Yes   No

RESULTS

If you answered yes mostly to questions 1 to 10, you are likely an indigo child!
Indigo children were usually born between the 1940s and 1979. Indigos are
intelligent and rebellious. They are often unable to conform to dysfunctional
situations at home, work, or school. Indigos want to tear down systems that
do not work well or are corrupt. They are creative, and they tend to get
bored easily.

If you answered yes mostly to questions 11 to 19, you are likely a crystal child!
Crystal children were born between 1970 and 1990. Crystals are intuitive
and spiritually aware. They are imaginative and creative. Crystals tend to be
extremely empathetic and sensitive. Despite their easygoing nature, crystals
often suffer with anxiety. Many crystals are late to speak and are musically
inclined. Crystals are often sensitive to chemicals, foods, medications, and
the environment.

If you answered yes mostly to questions 20 to 30, you are likely a rainbow
child! Rainbow children are the third generation of souls that have come to
help humanity evolve; they were born in the 1990s through the 2000s. Rainbows are resilient, and they recover from negative emotions or situations

easily. Rainbows have strong wills and tend not to care about what others think of them. They are much more fluid in their views than earlier generations. They are great manifesters, and are said to be the first generation born on the ninth dimension: the dimension of the collective unconscious.

Take a moment to reflect on your results for this exercise. Answer the following questions.

1. Are you an indigo, crystal, or rainbow child? Does this surprise you? Why, or why not?

_____

_____

2. Does this information help you understand yourself better? In what ways?

_____

_____

3. Will this information change the way you do things in your day-to-day life? If so, what do you think will be different?

_____

_____

_____

4. How can you integrate this information so it provides you with a sense of purpose? (Examples: continue reading about it, start a spiritual practice.)

_____

_____

5. If you aren't an indigo, crystal, or rainbow child, how do you think the information about all three can still help you as a fellow empath?

_____

_____

LIVE AND LOVE YOUR EMPATHIC LIFE

The empath's life is an adventure filled with exploration, unfathomable personal growth, and endless expansion. You are gifted with the ability to perform magic that is written about in books. You have psychic powers that can be studied and strengthened. You are naturally warm and kind, and, knowingly or not, your presence here is healing to the world around you. You are at one with nature, and you allow it to soothe you. You can feel the emotions of others, and you use this information when you choose to.

Empathic people regularly heal their families of dysfunction. When you honor your sensitivities, you stop the patterns of addiction, abuse, neglect, or other dysfunction that may have persisted for generations.

As empaths, we volunteered ourselves, and we came here to raise the vibration of the planet and the people. We are warriors, here to remind others to live from their hearts.

You Truly Are a Superhero!

Here are some questions that will help you focus on the amazing gifts that are unique to you.

1. In what way(s) has your empathy helped you? In what way(s) has your empathy helped others?

_____

_____

_____

2. How has your intuition benefited you? List any specific events that were impacted by your intuition.

_____

_____

_____

3. What empath powers are you most proud of?

_____

_____

_____

4. Which of the clairs (see page 7) are you most excited about strengthening?

_____

_____

_____

5. If there were no limits to how you used your gifts, what is one thing that you would use them to do?

_____

_____

_____

Breathing Is Everything

Every empath needs to learn and practice diaphragmatic breathing. This type of breathing should be used every time you meditate, use grounding techniques, practice energy medicine, or mindfully move your body. I do not exaggerate when I say that diaphragmatic breathing changed my life, and the lives of my coaching clients. I placed this section in chapter seven because I do believe that diaphragmatic breathing is necessary for an empath to thrive.

The following diaphragmatic breathing technique is an easy and effective way to get grounded, reduce anxiety and/or panic, decrease stress and overwhelm, eliminate other people's emotions, and regulate your physical body. Here are the steps:

1. Lie on your back on a flat surface with your knees bent. You can use a pillow under your knees and/or head for comfort. Place your right hand on your upper chest, and your left hand over your belly button. This will allow you to feel your diaphragm move as you breathe.
2. Breathe in slowly through your nose so that your stomach moves out against your hand. The hand on your chest should remain as still as possible.
3. Tighten your stomach muscles, letting them fall inward as you exhale through your mouth. The hand on your upper chest should remain relatively still.
4. Breathe deeply, using the diaphragm and stomach muscles, for five minutes. If you notice yourself getting dizzy, take a break and come back to the technique when you feel steady.

Practice diaphragmatic breathing for five minutes every day. As you practice, you may notice that this type of breathing becomes more natural. You might even discover yourself breathing this way outside of deliberate breath work.

In the Resources section, I have included a link to a video that demonstrates this breathing technique.

DEEPER PRACTICE: FREQUENCY, EMOTION, AND THE LAW OF ATTRACTION

Our emotional state is an exact translation of the frequency at which we vibrate. Higher-frequency emotional states include love, joy, excitement, and gratitude. Low-frequency states are those like anger, fear, and hopelessness.

According to a universal law called the law of attraction, things that vibrate at the same frequency gravitate together. This means that your emotional state and frequency will bring into your life people, material objects, and events that are a match to your frequency.

The law of attraction is one reason that empaths need to pay close attention to their emotional state, and to let go of emotions that are not their own. You are not just a sponge, but also a beacon. You are capable not just of picking up other people's frequencies, but of emitting frequencies, too, and you have a choice about what frequencies you wish to put out into the universe.

The more deliberately you choose your frequency, the less you will passively absorb the frequency, and emotion, of others. If you focus on how poorly you feel, you will remain under that dark cloud. If you focus instead on gratitude and positivity, eventually the cloud will depart and the sun will shine down on you again.

KEY LESSONS AND REFLECTION

→ Empaths are souls who volunteered to come here and heal people and the earth.

→ When we regularly practice the techniques that make us feel grounded, we shift from surviving to thriving.

→ Whether you are helping the world consciously or not, it makes no difference. It is your energy, not your behavior, that is healing the world.

→ When you honor your sensitivities, you stop the patterns of addiction, abuse, neglect, or other dysfunction that may have persisted for generations.

Reflection Questions

1. What were you most surprised about in this chapter?

_____

_____

2. Do you identify with the indigo, crystal, or rainbow children? If so, which of their characteristics sounded most like you?

_____

_____

3. What can you do that will help you remember how special and unique you are?

_____

_____

4. How do you plan to keep your frequency high?

_____

_____

Resources

CHAPTER 2: EMPATH IN THE WORLD

For a vast amount of information on being an empath, check out the website of the world's leading empath researcher, psychiatrist Judith Orloff, MD: drjudithorloff.com.

Common Ego. "Understanding the Gray Rock Method." YouTube, March 13, 2020. Available at YouTube/4EXxzYZLG6w.

Here are three books on developing boundaries, each with a specific niche:

Cloud, Henry, and John Townsend. *Boundaries in Dating: Making Dating Work*. 1st ed. Grand Rapids, MI: Zondervan, 2000.

Cloud, Henry, and John Townsend. *Boundaries with Kids: When to Say Yes, How to Say No*. 1st ed. Grand Rapids, MI: Zondervan, 1998.

Katherine, Anne. *Where to Draw the Line: How to Set Healthy Boundaries Every Day*. Orig. ed. New York: Fireside, 2000.

CHAPTER 3: EMPATH RELATIONSHIPS

Beattie, Melody. *Codependent No More: How to Stop Controlling Others and Start Caring for Yourself*. Center City, MN: Hazelden Publishing, 1992.

Lancer, Darlene. *Conquering Shame and Codependency: 8 Steps to Freeing the True You*. Center City, MN: Hazelden Publishing, 2014.

Northrup, Christiane. *Dodging Energy Vampires: An Empath's Guide to Evading Relationships That Drain You and Restoring Your Health and Power*. Carlsbad, CA: Hay House, 2018.

Vitale, Joe, and Ihaleakala Hew Len, *Zero Limits: The Secret Hawaiian System for Wealth, Health, Peace, and More*. Hoboken, NJ: John Wiley & Sons, 2007.

CHAPTER 4: THE EMPATH FAMILY

Day, Nicole. "Feeling Check-In" charts for children. *He's Extraordinary: Tools for Raising an Extraordinary Person* (blog). Available at Hes-extraordinary.com/downloads/feelings -check-in.

Eden, Donna. *Energy Medicine: Balancing Your Body's Energies for Optimal Health, Joy, and Vitality*. Revised and enlarged edition. New York: Jeremy P. Tarcher, 2008.

Ortner, Nick. *The Tapping Solution: A Revolutionary System for Stress-Free Living*. Carlsbad, CA: Hay House, 2013.

Ortner, Nick. *The Tapping Solution for Parents, Children, and Teenagers: How to Let Go of Excessive Stress, Anxiety, and Worry and Raise Happy, Healthy, Resilient Families*. Carlsbad, CA: Hay House, 2018.

The Tapping Solution. "How to Tap with Jessica Ortner: Emotional Freedom Technique Informational Video." YouTube. April 11, 2013. Available at YouTube/pAclBdj2OZU.

For more about Donna Eden and her energy medicine techniques, see her website, Eden Energy Medicine (EdenEnergyMedicine.com).

CHAPTER 5: EMPATH AT WORK

Wayofmastery. "Laughter Meditation." YouTube. August 11, 2011. Available at YouTube/sReREWoNyYY.

There are many groups of people who regularly participate in group laughing sessions all over the world. To find one in your area, check out the World Laughter Tour (WorldLaughterTour.com) or Meetup (Meetup.com).

For a short laughter practice, see the following article: Melissa Eisler, "Laughter Meditation: 5 Healing Benefits and a 10-Minute Practice." The Chopra Center, March 10, 2017. Available online at chopra.com/articles/laughter-meditation-5-healing-benefits-and-a-10-minute-practice.

CHAPTER 6: EMPATH SELF-CARE

Judith Orloff. "Dr. Orloff's Empath Support Community." Private Facebook Group. Available online at Facebook.com/groups/929510143757438.

This video will teach you step by step how to make your own orgonite: Hopegirl Youtube, "How We Make Our Orgone Step by Step Guide." YouTube, November 14, 2017. Available at YouTube/c8Zqx-k6AQ0.

For more detailed information on orgonite, see Georg Ritschl, "Orgone Energy—A Breakthrough That Has Already Happened—GLOBAL BEM conference Nov 2012." YouTube, March 27, 2013. Available at YouTube/nwxKB9IY3Js.

Eight Pieces. "Qigong Full 20-Minute Daily Routine." YouTube, January 7, 2018. Available at YouTube/cwlvTcWR3Gs.

Master Song Kung Fu. "Tai Chi Step by Step for Beginners Training Session 1." YouTube, April 8, 2020. Available at YouTube/NsZaY-EMpiA.

SarahBethYoga. "15 Minute Morning Yoga for Beginners." YouTube, March 17, 2017. Available at YouTube/m756Gz8de4M.

CHAPTER 7: EMPATH THRIVING

Michigan Medicine. "Diaphragmatic Breathing Demonstration from Michigan Medicine." YouTube, January 23, 2019. Available at YouTube/UB3tSaiEbNY. This video shows what diaphragmatic breathing looks like.

References

Acho, Jackie. "A Good Day's Work Requires Empathy." TEDx Talks. December 6, 2014. Available online at YouTube/x6dyrmHljao.

Anticole, Matt. "Is Radiation Dangerous?" TED-Ed. March 2016. Video directed by Tinmouse Animation Studio. Available online at ted.com/talks/matt_anticole_is_radiation_dangerous.

"Aromatherapy with Essential Oils." National Cancer Institute. Published online: October 25, 2019. Created: October 24, 2005. Available at NCBI.nlm.nih.gov/books /NBK65874. Accessed May 26, 2020.

Aron, Elaine. *The Highly Sensitive Person: How to Survive and Thrive When the World Overwhelms You*. New York: Broadway Books, reprint edition, 1997.

Breus, Michael J. "How Can Binaural Beats Help You Sleep Better?" *Psychology Today*, October 11, 2018. Available at psychologytoday.com/us/blog/sleep-newzzz/201810 /how-can-binaural-beats-help-you-sleep-better.

Burleson, Mary H., Wenda R. Trevathan, and Michael Todd. "In the Mood for Love or Vice Versa? Exploring the Relations among Sexual Activity, Physical Affection, Affect, and Stress in the Daily Lives of Mid-aged Women." *Archives of Sexual Behavior* (June 2007). doi: 10.1007/s10508-006-9071-1.

Cannon, Dolores. *Three Waves of Volunteers and the New Earth*. Huntsville, AR: Ozark Mountain Publishing, 2011.

Chevalier, G., G. Melvin, and T. Barsotti. "One-Hour Contact with the Earth's Surface (Grounding) Improves Inflammation and Blood Flow—A Randomized, Double-Blind, Pilot Study." *Health* 7, no. 8 (August 2015): 1022–59. doi: 10.4236/health.2015.78119.

Chignell, Barry. "Seven Benefits of Having Plants in Your Office." CIPHR. February 19, 2018. Available at ciphr.com/advice/plants-in-the-office. Accessed May 24, 2020.

Cross, R., R. Rebele, and A. Grant. "Collaborative Overload." *American Journal of Lifestyle Medicine* 10, no. 4 (July–August 2016): 262–67. Available at hbr.org/2016/01/collaborative-overload.

Ditzen, B., I. D. Neumann, G. Bodenmann, B. von Dawans, R. A. Turner, U. Ehlert, and M. Heinrichs. "Effects of Different Kinds of Couple Interaction on Cortisol and Heart Rate Responses to Stress in Women." *Psychoneuroendocrinology* 32, no. 5 (June 2007): 565–74.

Dowden, Craig. "Forget Ethics Training: Focus on Empathy." *Financial Post*. Last updated February 27, 2015. Available at business.financialpost.com/executive/c-suite/forget-ethics-training-focus-on-empathy.

Emmons, Robert A., and Michael E. McCullough. "Why Gratitude Is Good." *Journal of Personality and Social Psychology* 84, no. 2 (Feb 2003): 377–89.

Frank et al. (2013). "Susceptibility to Emotional Contagion for Negative Emotions Improves Detection of Smile Authenticity." *Journal of Human Neuroscience* 32: 225–39.

Friedman, Lauren, and Kevin Loria. "11 Scientific Reasons You Should Be Spending More Time Outside." *Business Insider*, April 22, 2016. Available at businessinsider.com/scientific-benefits-of-nature-outdoors-2016-4?op=1. Accessed May 24, 2020.

Fry, Richard. "The Share of Americans Living without a Partner Has Increased, Especially among Young Adults." Pew Research Center: FactTank: News in the Numbers. October 11, 2017. Available online at pewresearch.org/fact-tank/2017/10/11/the-share-of-americans-living-without-a-partner-has-increased-especially-among-young-adults.

Garcia-Argibay, Miguel, Miguel A. Santed, and José M. Reales. "Efficacy of Binaural Auditory Beats in Cognition, Anxiety, and Pain Perception: A Meta-analysis." *Psychological Research* 83 (2019): 357–92. Published online August 2, 2018. Available at link.springer.com/article/10.1007/s00426-018-1066-8.

Ghaly, Maurice, and Dale Teplitz. "The Biologic Effects of Grounding the Human Body during Sleep as Measured by Cortisol Levels and Subjective Reporting of Sleep, Pain, and Stress." *Journal of Alternative and Complementary Medicine* 10, no. 5 (October 2004): 767–76. doi: 10.1089/acm.2004.10.767.

Hansen, Eric M., J. H. Eklund, A. Hallén, C. S. Bjurhager, E. Norrström, A. Viman, and E. Stocks. "Does Feeling Empathy Lead to Compassion Fatigue or Compassion Satisfaction? The Role of Time Perspective." *Journal of Psychology: Interdisciplinary and Applied* 152, no. 8 (October 2018): 630–45. Accessed April 2, 2020. doi: 10.1080/00223980.2018.1495170.

Heerwagen, Judith. "The Benefits of Plants in the Workplace." *Work Design Magazine*. n.d. Available at workdesign.com/2012/07/the-benefits-of-plants-in-the-workplace. Accessed May 24, 2020.

Jäger, R., M. Purpura, and M. Kingsley. "Phospholipids and Sport Performance." *Journal of International Sports Nutrition* 4, no. 5 (2007). Accessed on April 1, 2020. DOI.org/10.1186/1550-2783-4-5.

Jameson, Stephanie. *The Happy Empath's Workbook*. Berkeley, CA: Ulysses Press, 2018.

Jeon, Hyeonjin, and Seung-Hwan Lee. "From Neurons to Social Beings: Short Review of the Mirror Neuron System Research and Its Socio-Psychological and Psychiatric Implications." *Clinical Psychopharmacology and Neuroscience* 16, no. 1 (February 2018): 18–31. doi: 10.9758/cpn.2018.16.1.18.

Kaszuba-Zwoińska J., J. Gremba, B. Gałdzińska-Calik, K. Wójcik-Piotrowicz, and P. J. Thor. "Electromagnetic Field Induced Biological Effects in Humans." *Przeglad Lekarski* 72, no.11 (2015): 636–41. PMID: 27012122.

Ko, H. J., C. H. Youn, S. H. Kim, and S. Y. Kim. "Effect of Pet Insects on the Psychological Health of Community-Dwelling Elderly People: A Single-Blinded, Randomized, Controlled Trial." *Gerontology* 62, no. 2 (September 18, 2015): 200-9. doi: 10.1159/000439129.

Kross, Ethan, et al. "Facebook Use Predicts Declines in Subjective Well-Being in Young Adults." *PLoS One* 8, no. 8 (August 14, 2013). Accessed on April 15, 2020 at DOI.org/10.1371/journal.pone.0069841.

Kujath, Joanna. "Top 5 Nutrients for Highly Sensitive People." YouTube. June 24, 2016. Available at YouTube/hl1VRGk_6ZY.

Mao, Gen-Xiang, et al. "Therapeutic Effect of Forest Bathing on Human Hypertension in the Elderly." *Journal of Cardiology* 60 (5–6) (September 2012). doi: 10.1016/j.jjcc.2012.08.003.

McMakin, Carolyn. *The Resonance Effect*. Berkeley, CA: North Atlantic Books, 2017.

Miller, Anna Medaris. "Grounding: Hype or Healing?" *U.S. News & World Report*, November 3, 2017. Available online at health.usnews.com/wellness/articles/2017-11-03/grounding-hype-or-healing. Accessed May 24, 2020.

Milner, Corri. *Empaths on Their Soul Path*. Self-published, 2017.

Northrup, Christiane. *Dodging Energy Vampires: An Empath's Guide to Evading Relationships That Drain You and Restoring Your Health and Power*. 2nd edition. Carlsbad, CA: Hay House, 2019.

Northrup, Christiane. "You or Them: Reclaiming Your Health from Energy Vampires Before It's Too Late." March 12, 2018. Hay House. Available at YouTube.com/watch?v=Jz5DIDSDFRo.

Orloff, Judith. *The Empath's Survival Guide*. Boulder, CO: Sounds True Publishing, 2018.

Padmanabhan, R., A. J. Hildreth, and D. Laws. "A Prospective, Randomised, Controlled Study Examining Binaural Beat Audio and Pre-operative Anxiety in Patients Undergoing General Anaesthesia for Day Case Surgery." *Anaesthesia* (July 7, 2005). Accessed March 24, 2020. doi: 10.1111/j.1365-2044.2005.04287.x.

Sagioglou, C., and T. Greitemeyer. "Facebook's Emotional Consequences: Why Facebook Causes a Decrease in Mood and Why People Still Use It." *Computers in Human Behavior* 35 (June 2014): 359–63. doi: 10.1016.j.chb.2014.03.003.

ScienceNOW. "Mirror Neurons." *NOVA* (PBS, January 5, 2005). Video available online at YouTube/Xmx1qPyo8Ks. Transcript available online at pbs.org/wgbh/nova /video/mirror-neurons.

"Stress Relief from Laughter? It's No Joke." Mayo Clinic. April 5, 2019. Available at MayoClinic.org/healthy-lifestyle/stress-management/in-depth/stress-relief/art -20044456. Accessed May 24, 2020.

Vitale, Joe, and Ihaleakala Hew Len. *Zero Limits: The Secret Hawaiian System for Wealth, Health, Peace, and More.* Hoboken, NJ: John Wiley & Sons, 2007.

Index

Acknowledgments

A very large thank-you goes out to my mother, Connie Carpenter. She shopped, cooked, ran errands, and cleaned for me, like only a mother would, as I researched and wrote. Mom, I would never have been able to write a book during a pandemic while also running a therapy practice and experiencing a breakup. As usual, you were my saving grace. Thank you, and I love you.

I want to give a big thank-you to both Seth Schwartz and Amy Rost, two of the editors of this book. Both Seth and Amy went through the manuscript with a keen sense for what the book needed, all the while being thoughtful and kind. This book would not be what it is without their hard work and dedication. Amy, in particular, knows the subject matter so well that she was able to add valuable information that I would have missed. I cannot thank you both enough for your hard work.

Additionally, I would like to thank Joe Cho and Callisto Media for the opportunity to write *The Empath's Workbook*. Writing a book has been a dream of mine for a long time, but it seemed like too big an undertaking until I was presented with this particular opportunity. I was honored even to be considered as the author. Joe, you helped me in every way you could to be selected as the author, and I will be forever grateful.

About the Author

Krista Carpenter, MS, is an intuitive life coach who specializes in working with empathic people. Krista received her master's of science degree in counseling in 2003 from Texas A&M University. She received a bachelor of science degree in psychology from the University of Wisconsin in 2000. Krista runs Happy Empath Coaching, where the focus is always on developing her clients' strengths in a way that allows them to feel empowered and in charge of their lives. Krista supports her clients' growth as they develop their intuitive gifts, find happiness, and live the life of their dreams.

CPSIA information can be obtained
at www.ICGtesting.com
Printed in the USA
JSHW051615081120
9365JS00002B/2